A Healer's Journey to Healing

PORCIA MANN

13TH & JOAN

For permission requests, write to the publisher, addressed "Attention: Permissions Coordinator," 205 N. Michigan Avenue, Suite #810, Chicago, IL 60601. 13th & Joan books may be purchased for educational, business or sales promotional use. For information, please email the Sales Department at sales@13thandjoan.com.

Printed in the U. S. A.

First Printing, October 2022.

Library of Congress Cataloging-in-Publication Data has been applied for.

ISBN: 978-1-953156-91-4

ENDORSEMENTS

I often say, "Don't rush through the journey because it holds all the good stuff." After reading this book, my advice to you is, "Don't rush through pages prying for information instead, take your time so that you can digest the wisdom that is subtly woven into the text." This book feels like a weekend at Big Mama's house. The delicate stroke of Porcia's pen is like Big Mama's story-filled hand caressing your head while it lays in her lap. It is so honest that you don't judge the naivety, you empathize with it, you can visualize the growth, and almost taste the maturation. The wisdom sprinkled throughout this book by way of the stories Porcia discloses are sure to change your outlook forever. After reading this, you'll fire your judgment and hire compassion full time because Porcia's journey is proof that it doesn't have to be pretty to be effective. Get your notepad, take notes, and don't feel bad for talking back to the pages you read… I did it too. ENJOY.

Joshua D. Blocker
Actor, Author, CEO of JuJo Publishing Co.

Porcia does a fantastic job showing the chaotic thoughts of a young woman navigating her life while interweaving the wisdom and lessons of her current self. Her use of very specific details truly helps readers to see the world through her eyes. At its core, this book is TRUTH… in all of its forms. You can't help but to be encouraged by this vulnerable journey.

Tiffany Mann

DEDICATION:

To my daughters: Ashton, Maddison, Kennedy, and Rhileey…

I have been a student and you, girls, have been the most gracious teachers. Thank you for loving me the way yall do.

PAIN IS THE LIGHT. PAIN IS INSIGHT. WE
KNEEL HERE. WE HEAL HERE. WE OPEN
OUR HEARTS TO THE HEAVENS.

SAMANTHA SMITH

FOREWORD

Laporcia Deshon Mann was born on July 26, 1986, in Cleburne, Texas to David Mann, Deshon Gill, and bonus mom, Tamela Mann weighing 6 pounds and 5 ounces. She entered this world as a beautiful bouncing brown baby girl. She was raised in the fear and admonition of the Lord with strong foundational principles that has carried her far in life.

This book has been birthed out of her share of trials, tribulations, adversities, hurts, pains, and rejections. I welcome you to her journey of experiences and healing.

After high school, Porcia birthed three beautiful daughters, Madison, Kennedy and Rhileey, who are truly gifts from God. She overcame relationship barriers through prayer and determination. Fortunately some of the relationships have been preserved because Unity and Support is God's will. All children need their families because it takes a village to raise a child. God has given Porcia the strength and faith to get up, stand tall and look face to face with every giant that has tried to hinder and stop her, and fight for her life. Was it easy? No. Healing is a process and every individual handles and responds to their trials and adversities differently.

Porcia has encountered levels of pain that has molded her into the warrior, champion, and vessel of healing that she is today. She is on an assignment on this Earth as God orders her steps to be a blessing and inspiration to all who will read this book.

Although she has made tremendous progress in her life, she is still under construction, growing and evolving daily in order to be a Productive Woman, Mother, Mentor, and Community and Global Leader letting the nations know that you can make it if you keep fighting the good fight of Faith.

Porcia's process of healing has come with sleepless nights, tears, and consistent praying and meditation. Proverbs 22:6 says: "Train up a child in the way he should go and when he is old he shall not depart from it."

As I close out this Foreword, I want to leave you with this note: love yourself! Embrace Yourself! Discover your true identity in Christ and in this world! Execute and carry out your visions and dreams! God loves you and so do I. Move forward with your goals and dreams because we have all had our share of pain, but there is medicine for the journey, spiritual and natural medicine that will strengthen each one of you. Storms will come, but my readers, we must learn to dance in the rain and keep trusting God daily, because He is the God of Miracles if we only believe. Laporcia is a Survivor!

Thank You, Jesus!
Deshon Chambers Gill

CONTENTS

Dear Reader,

To be living in an era where women create and share art that will heal generations is such a dope feeling. I've always had a soft spot for women with rocky life journeys. Those are the women I would like to speak to.

To the woman who has to dance to feed her child, you are special and you have a purpose.

To the promiscuous girl who feels like your body is all you have to offer, YOU ARE WORTH MORE THAN GOLD, SIS!

To the woman who resorts to shoplifting because she can't afford diapers and her pride won't let her ask for help, your breakthrough is closer than you think. Don't fold.

I was once all of these women. The day I started loving myself is the day I realized that I'm really a force to be reckoned with. Past mistakes no longer define who I am. They are what I did and not who I am. I am a mother, a daughter, a sister, a friend, and a healing vessel.

If you have anyone in your life that constantly reminds you of your past mistakes, it stops today. If they love you, they'll respect your boundaries and your relationships will flourish. If they buck back, you may have to detach for a while, but please know that things will always work out the way they are supposed to. Set boundaries. Require others to respect those boundaries. Be patient with yourself and your loved ones because, to be honest, we are all just trying to figure it out.

Love,
Porcia

INTRODUCTION

WHEN I first started writing this book everyone's names were changed and the stories were only *loosely* based on my life. I really wanted to hide behind these stories because they are uncomfortable, but I realized that transparency and truth is a must for me. Some of my most sacred stories were written in the middle of chaos, and to water them down didn't feel authentic to me. I promised myself that if I'm going to do this, I need to do it my way.

My mother and father weren't a couple when I was born, but I was conceived in love. The type of love my parents shared may have been fueled by temporary feelings, but still, there was love there. At some point in the 80s, two souls came together and created me. I must admit that growing up with 3 parents made for a confusing start on this journey. My dad married my bonus mother when I was only a toddler and the three of them set out on this co-parenting journey together.

The foundation of who I am consists of my grandmother's prayers, my mother's teachings, and my father's wisdom. The goal was never to mirror my parents' lives, it was always to take what was instilled in me and build upon that in my own way according to God's purpose for my life. I realize that I could have chosen a different path. I could've chosen the path that my parents envisioned for me, I could've followed my peers down their paths, I could've even followed the path of failure that was paved for me just because of my mistakes. Instead,

I chose to do my life my way. It has taken me almost 7 years to share these moments, and while I am very anxious about sharing it with you, I'm walking in boldness and truth. As you sit down to read my story, I want you to open your heart and mind. This book isn't a blueprint to life, these are my experiences. God is the only person in control of your destiny. Never forget that.

I was raised in a family of women who made things happen and that stuck with me my whole life. Over time I learned that our stories aren't solely for us. I understand that now. With much prayer and self-reflection, I am able to bare my soul to you. Every person that has entered my life was there for a reason. Their seasons may have been brief and their aftermath left me with more baggage than I needed to carry, but healing is *my* responsibility. The healer's journey is a treacherous road of highs and lows and it requires strength. It requires you to embrace every peak and valley experience. Once the dust settles you will see the beauty emerge. My hope is for you to experience the way it feels to be liberated and to walk in your life's purpose because it's truly remarkable.

Take a moment to really digest the sacred pieces of every story, because in many moments, I was writing from some very broken places. Healing will take place as you go through each season with me. My soul has housed butterflies and wounds too deep for words, but they're mine.

Chapter 1

THE BIG LITTLE TOWN

ITASCA, Texas is the heart and soul of who I am. The "big little town" is what the people there call it. My sister and I spent some time living here with my grandmother while my mother attended Prairie View A&M University.

My grandmother is a godly woman. The house that we resided in is where my mother and Aunt Princess were raised. There was a permanent foot trail lined with trees behind the house that led to a church. Bethlehem Baptist church was granny's second home and now that she had the responsibility of 5 small children, it became ours as well.

Me, my sister Nerra, and our 3 cousins spent our Saturday mornings getting our hair done to prepare for Sunday morning service. We'd line up at the sink and one by one granny would shampoo our hair, add some thick hair cholesterol, and finish it off with the most awful smelling vinegar. She would then braid it up to let it air dry. In between shampoos she would move over to the stove to fix a bite to eat for whoever was waiting to go next. I remember sitting on a stack of pillows and hearing her say, "come here, girl, so I can press this hair. Y'all can't be walking around here with your hair all nappy." She'd part the hair, gently grease my scalp, then go over it with the hot comb that she would pull from the eye of the kitchen stove. The sizzle was enough to make you think your ears were about to be burned off, but one cool blow from her lips and the smoke was gone. When she was finished I would look in the mirror to admire my neatly pressed hair.

Cornelia Ethel Dean Jarmon, my grandmother, is a staple in her community. She was a member of every board you could think of. On the board of the town cemetery program she made sure the cemetery was presentable at all times. But out of all the things she was involved in, one of my favorites was the nursing home ministry. She would take us girls to the local nursing center to interact with the elderly residents while she played a few hymns for them on the piano. This is where my love and deep reverence for the elderly started.

We walked the trail to church every Sunday morning. She prepared breakfast for us every time, and the mornings that we had to rush, she would stash bacon and biscuits in her bag that we would eat in the fellowship hall before service started. The longest Sundays were when something called The Federation of Churches would take place. Not only did we have to attend Sunday morning services, but we would take a break and then by 3:00 we were headed to the church across town for their service.

We would all pile into the pew next to the piano so my grandmother could keep an eye on us while she belted out *This Little Light of Mine*. Most of the time we would get to lay across each other's lap and catch a quick nap. She didn't make us wake up because we were small children. She understood that. Our Sundays were long, but they were special.

Now my paternal grandmother, I was too young to remember life with her, but the stories I've heard are etched in my memory.

Sandra Etta Mann was and still is the most resilient woman I know. She raised five boys as a single mother and she still held it together. From what I heard, she was elated to hear about the birth of her first granddaughter. When I made my way into this world I was told that I was surrounded by nothing but love. Both sides of my family would begin to slowly form the village that would raise me. At Granny Sandra's house, I had my own closet with a stylish wardrobe and a pair of ruffle socks to match every dress.

Granny Sandra was also very territorial. After I was born she told my mother that I would be calling *her* mama, and my mother would be called by her name. I was her baby. My mother was not the petty kind of woman, but she was strong, so she let Granny have it. "Sandra, this is my child and she will not be calling *you* mama." I laugh now at this story because when my granny tells it, she has this serious look on her face as if my mom was out of line! I can't blame her though, because after having five boys, a little girl coming into the picture was special to her.

My mom let me go visit my father and grandmother as often as they wanted. The craziest story I have been told about their co-parenting was the time my mother had to call the police to get me back. My grandmother was going to work so I would stay home with my dad. Apparently, I had been there for a couple of weeks already and my mother was ready for me to come home. She drove the 45 minutes from Itasca to Arlington, TX to get me because my dad and grand-mother didn't bring me back like they agreed on.

When my dad comes to the door she says to him, "I have let you spend more than enough time with her, it's time for her to come home." The story goes that my dad closed the door in her face because there was no way that he was letting me go back this time. Five minutes go by and there is another knock. When he opens the door this time, my mother is there with a dozen police officers who informed my dad that he had 15 minutes to get me dressed or there would be problems. My dad said he closed the door, quickly wrapped me up, and had me outside in less than five minutes, forget fifteen!

Like all new parents, there were hiccups along the way, but they eventually found a system that worked. My bonus mom was a vital part of my early years as well. So much so that she was present at the hospital for my birth. My siblings and I joke about this all of the time because back then they were just "friends," but we all knew what was up. My mother and father were no longer in a relationship when I was born, but I was conceived out of love. They all made the decision to put their feelings aside for my best interest. My bonus mom would make the drive to Itasca with my father to get me and there were times when she would come spend alone time with me. She really put in the effort to build a relationship with me at an early age.

Living with my grandma, Cornelia, was special, but it was hard not having my mother around all the time.

Not only was my mother gorgeous, she was intelligent.

Although she was focused and working hard in school, she didn't just go away and forget about us. She visited home often and she was very present in our lives. No parent or grandparent was perfect, but they were all working together to make it work.

During my mother's time away, she stumbled upon the "love of her life." One day she drove down from Houston to let us know that she was engaged to be married and that we would be moving five hours away. Excitement was the first emotion I felt because I had missed my mama. We would be moving to our own place with our own rooms and we would be a family! We were off to start our new life in the city.

My mom and Mr.'s wedding took place on the campus of Prairie View A&M university. Nerra and I were the flower girls, we wore long white ruffle dresses and our hair was up in French buns. I was never a fan of the ruffle dresses with the matching socks look, but my mother loved it.

There was so much food and love in the room. My mama had the tallest cake I had ever seen in my life and the groom's cake was made of all chocolate. My mama was such a beautiful bride and she looked genuinely happy. It felt like a fairytale. They said their "I do's," people sang, and just like that we were part of a brand-new family.

After the wedding, I remember getting into Mr.'s two-door car. There was a long trail of balloons attached to the back as we drove off into the sunset. Everybody was snapping pictures and blowing bubbles and everything seemed like it was going to be alright.

We didn't stay in Houston long, we moved to Waller, TX to Bayou Bend Apartments shortly after the wedding. Our new home was a two-bedroom apartment. Nerra and I shared a room and our mother would hang positive affirmations on every wall in our room. She was very big on making sure our confidence and self-esteem were high. Two twin beds were neatly made on each side of the room. On our dressers were folders full of papers with scriptures and all of the fruit of the spirit. Over the next few months we would be drilled on these principles.

Holleman Elementary became our new school. I have always been a quiet person so I didn't make many new friends at my new school right away, but I was okay. There are two things I remember about this school: the school song and Christmas. My obsession with the holiday season started here. Christmas parties were magical back then. Our classrooms were decorated from top to bottom. We had hot chocolate, Christmas cookies, and the teachers dressed up in festive clothes. I will always remember the feeling.

Everything seemed to be great; I was in love with our new life. For the most part we had a pretty normal childhood. Just like my grandmother, my mother was deeply rooted in the church. We attended every Sunday morning church service, bible study, choir rehearsal, and church conference there was to attend. I could quote the books of the bible forward and backwards and I knew more scriptures than most adults.

Everything *seemed* like it was going to be alright, but a few months into living with my new stepdad, I soon found out that he was not the most pleasant person to live with. He was very strict and militant. Now I get it, structure is necessary, I'll give you that, but he made us feel *bad* for doing *normal* kid stuff.

Since he was a musician he thought it was a good idea to force singing onto my sister and I. Now I'll be the first to tell you, despite coming from a musically-inclined family, God did not intend for me to be a singer. So what made Mr. think that he could magically *make* me a singer? Nerra and I would spend hours in front of his keyboard attempting to push out notes that were simply not there, and each wrong note brought a badass swing from his thick leather belt. I was getting hit all the time because I CAN NOT SING! Mama would drill us with scriptures and then he would teach us all these new songs that we would recite at different churches. I appreciated my mother for keeping us rooted in the word, but I HATED being in front of all those people, let alone singing in front of them!

One day after dinner my mother had given us instructions to clean our room before she came in to read our daily affirmations and do bible study with us. As soon as I stepped in the hall from cleaning our room, I saw Mr.; I immediately knew he was about to mess up our day. He motioned for us to come back into the kitchen, get the food out of the trash can, and finish eating it. He always talked about his hatred for wasted food, but he had never gone so far as to tell Nerra and I to get food out of the trashcan and eat it! My mama looked so defeated when he told us to do this. Normally she would comply with what he was saying, but this day, he had her all types of messed up.

Although mama could hold her own, no woman is a match for a man. There were times when she and Mr. would fight and I would feel helpless because I was so young. Our normal routine for these fights were that we would go in our room and pray because she would be hollering during the beatings. He would use his hands *and* his belts, which was crazy because my mama was a full-grown woman. My sister and I wanted to help her, but we were so tiny and we didn't stand a chance against Mr... So we just waited. Almost every time he was abusive he left immediately after. As soon as we heard the front door close, we slowly crept into the hallway to go check on her.

"I'll be out in a minute, girls," she would tell us. But that was never enough to stop us because we knew that more than likely she was hurt. I opened the door to her room to find her sitting on the side of the bed defeated. I went into the restroom to get her a tissue to clean up the blood, then Nerra and I would just sit with her. The silence was loud.

There aren't a lot of things that I remember vividly from back then, but there are certain days I'll never forget. One day, Mr. and his family planned a family day out for everyone. My mother was a very neat woman. She was always put together. This day she had on a denim overall dress with a plain white shirt underneath. Her hair was neatly pulled back into a ponytail and her skin was flawless. "Today is going to be a good day," I thought to myself. Mama and Mr. seemed to be getting along pretty good, and It just *felt* like a good day.

We were in the car going down the freeway, when I heard her tell him, "Slow down." Now what did she do that for? Of course, asking, or even telling, someone to slow down is no big thing, but he was the type of man to make a mountain out of a molehill.

"Do you want to drive?" He asked her. She turned to the window and shut down. It was as if her brain, or her trauma, told her to disengage, because she knew where it could go. I bet she was thinking, "let's not ruin this day for the girls."

But just that small argument turned into one of the biggest fights I've ever seen between the two of them. He looked out his rear-view mirror and signaled to switch lanes. I was thinking, "thank you, GOD, we are almost there," because he was pulling over. We pulled over on the side of a busy freeway, he threw the car in park and told my mom to get out. "Get out?" She turned around to look at us and I was giving her a, "Please don't get out of this car" look. She said, "Why would you put us out in the middle of the freeway?"

"Not them, just you," he said. My heart sank and my sister and I both started to cry, "Mama, please don't get out."

"Let's just go home." We didn't even care about going to six flags anymore; we just wanted to go home. He started to become a little more agitated and he yelled at her, "GET OUT NOW!" Reluctantly she swung open her car door, grabbed her purse, and stepped out. Before she could even close the door, he sped away. "There is no way we are going to survive living with this man," I immediately thought to myself. I was a kid, so in my mind that was the last time we would see mama. We pulled into this shopping mall and he told us to get out. All I kept thinking was, "I wonder if mama got hit by a car. Did someone give her a ride?" I hated him.

It was only about 15 minutes between Mr. putting her out of the car and us then seeing her at the spot the family was supposed to meet at. When we walked in I saw my mama standing there with Mr.'s brother. His ugly ass didn't even think to call anyone to help her or go back for her. He just went on with the day as if he didn't dump her out on the side of the freeway. He was the step dad from hell.

She pulled us to the side and apologized to us for having to witness that and she promised us the rest of the day would be fun.

In my mom's house, our business was *our* business, so there were things I didn't share with my dad because of this rule. My mother did the best that she could with my sister and I, but I felt like my dad and bonus mom could help her take care of me if she just told them what was happening in our home. Times were hard. I had to talk to my dad and bonus mom about the way I felt without my mom knowing. One day I found some change and went to the payphone to call my dad. I briefly told him how I had been feeling and his response was simply, "I'm on my way."

Houston, Texas was roughly 4 and a half hours from Mansfield, Texas. It seemed as though I blinked and my father was knocking at our apartment door.

I knew that when he came to get me that eventually I would have to come back home, unless we convinced my mother to let me move in with him.

I looked out the window and the car stopped at a Taco Bell. The first thing out of my bonus mom's mouth was, "baby, you can order whatever you want." It seems small, but that is when I officially knew that I was in a safe space, and I began to relax.

After I sat my dad and bonus mom down and asked them to let me move in with them, my dad knew he then had to convince my mom and it wasn't going to be easy. I wasn't privy to most of their conversations so I don't know what was said. I just put my plea in and crossed my fingers. In my heart I felt so bad for leaving Nerra there alone because we were so close. My mother found love in this man and not only did he let her down, he emotionally scarred us in the process. I was sad to leave my mom and my sister, but I knew it was something I needed to do.

My mother was a praying woman. She put deep thought into her decision and eventually, with much resistance and reluctance, she agreed to let me move in with my dad and bonus mom for good.

Shortly after I moved in with them, my mother divorced Mr. and her and Nerra moved back to Itasca.

Chapter 2

NEW SISTER ON THE BLOCK

My parents' house was a 3-bedroom home on a piece of land with more honeysuckle trees than I had ever seen. Tia, David, and I would climb the fence to see if we could reach some of the ones that hung down so we could indulge in the sweet nectar that these flowers produced. We would usually play in the backyard with each other, but some days we would help my dad mow the lawn or be inside helping my bonus mom cook. I knew from my early visits that I *had* to live here. My dad was nothing like my step dad. The dynamic of this home was completely different from what I had gotten used to with my mom and Mr., but like any place, it still had its flaws.

At my mom's house, she didn't allow us to speak negatively to each other in a serious nor joking way. She made sure Nerra and I were careful not to say certain things to one another, so I wasn't a big jokester. I took things to heart because that's how my mom and grandmother raised me. We didn't comment on each other's bodies or discuss each other's flaws. This wasn't the case at my dad and bonus mom's house. There was no limit to the things that were said and dressed up as a joke. I was very sensitive. One day my brother called me a goat and I cried so much. My dad was a comedian so quite naturally his junior followed in his footsteps. It was a joke, but because I was coming into this house a very fragile person who had been taught not to joke like that it hurt my feelings. I went to my parents about it and they told me I needed to get thicker skin. My brother became one of the reasons I was very insecure about my gap and my skin complexion. Every chance he got he was commenting on it. To add to that, when he got mad about something his go to thing was to remind me that his mom was not my mom. Looking back, that was typical for a newly blended family, but in the heat of the moment I was pissed. I guess he was just doing what little brothers typically do. Yet still, I would go to my parents and they would sit me down and tell me that these were just jokes and I needed to find something to say back to him. My comebacks started to be centered around his weight. He would call me black and I'd call him fat almost every time and that became the way we "loved" each other growing up. It was odd, but that was the dynamic of our relationship.

Tia is younger than both of us so she normally stayed out of arguments. She would chime in every now and then to stand up for me and remind David that we were all brothers and sisters, but for the most part she would let us go at it. Her and David were thick as thieves though. If they were having an argument I learned to stay out of it, otherwise they would turn on me. They always respected me as a big sister. The beginning of our sibling love started out rocky, but we eventually learned to lean on each other. Tia quickly became my favorite sibling on my dad's side because she really was my baby. I believe it had a lot to do with us sharing rooms because when we were supposed to be going to sleep at night, we would stay up talking. Sometimes we would go into David's room and do the most off the wall things. I convinced both of them that if we put toothpaste on the ceiling fan it would spin faster. I don't even know where that idea came from, but at the time it made sense to me. So there we were, standing on his bed smearing toothpaste all over the ceiling fan.

I didn't meet my sister Tiffany until she was five years old. My parents sat us down and said we would all be going to a park to meet her for the first time. I don't remember the full conversation we had, but I do remember making up in my mind that she would not come into this easily. I was the older sister, so anything I did, David and Tia were watching. Although I knew I needed to be a good role model, I failed miserably. Our first encounter wasn't at all pleasant. I remember pushing her down and David and Tia were watching. Yes, I was young, but even as a young girl I knew I had the responsibility of setting a good example.

The next time we saw Tiffany was when she came to stay at our house. Her and David were both middle children so they bumped heads a lot. I remember thinking to myself, "Ok, I need to be nice to her. If they see me being kind then I am almost sure they will follow suit." One day Tiffany and David were in one of their middle-child moods and he pulled the, "that's not yall's mom," card. I remember saying to him, "I was here before you anyway so technically she *was* my mom first." After that I pulled David and Tia into Tia's room and told them we needed to be nice to Tiffany. She only came to visit some weekends and I didn't want her experience with us to be bad. The situation was already awkward with the adults so I wanted us to try to keep it together on our end. We didn't pull it together overnight and become best friends all of a sudden, but we started to at least respect each other. We understood that we were all related regardless of who had different moms. Aside from the adolescent drama we had, I love all of my siblings. We were, and still are, in this for life.

Christmas was my bonus mom's favorite time of year and she always went all out with the decorations. I always looked forward to putting up the Christmas decorations and of course I was excited about the gifts. We all knew when It was time for Christmas shopping to begin because our parents would move through the house like secret agents. They would leave for hours and then we would hear the car pull up in the driveway and one of them would come inside and say, "everybody to your rooms and close the doors!" Of course we peeked into the hall to see them rushing to their bedroom with hundreds of bags from different stores, wrapping paper, tape, and everything else they needed to wrap the gifts. Christmas was magical in this house.

In the midst of adjusting to my new home life and enjoying the holidays, I also had to go to school. I started my 6th grade year in a new city at a new school. In school I kept to myself for the most part. Everybody there had been to school with each other since elementary, so best friend positions had already been filled. During recess I immediately noticed the different groups of people. In one corner were the preps or jocks, the goth kids had the back of the area on lock, and on the basketball court were most of the boys and one girl named Stacey. Every single day she would be the only girl on the court. I would think to myself, I would be so embarrassed to be the only girl out there. And even though in the beginning I was judging her on the low, before you knew it she had become one of my good friends. I had finally started to come out of my shell. And then, at the end of my 6th grade year, my parents told us we would be moving deeper into town and I would have to change schools...again. I wouldn't be going to middle school with the group of friends I had *just* made in 6th grade. I had to start all over again. I might as well have been a military kid.

My dad and bonus mom moved from one house to a two-story house and with each move things started to change. I noticed new

17

cars and life starting to progress for them. It was cool to see, but I only wanted two things. I wanted to live with them wherever they lived and I wanted my last name to match theirs.

We lived down the street from my new school so I would be walking with some other kids from the neighborhood. The first day of school was a mixture of feelings and emotions. I looked down at my schedule to see where my first class was and I was so confused. I stood beside my locker and attempted to look like I knew what was going on, so I didn't look like a nerd, but clearly that plan didn't work.

"You don't even know what you're looking at, girl!" I turned around to see this really tall light skinned guy standing beside me.

"I actually don't," I admitted.

"Lemme help you out. This is my school."

"Um, aren't you new to this school too? Are you a 7th grader or 8th?"

"That doesn't matter, do you want to get to class or not," he asked.

He had a point.

I wasn't even thinking about liking anyone, but I couldn't help but notice how cute he was.

"You must be popular."

"Something like that. I'm just nice," he said with a big smile.

"Yeah, I bet you are."

"Damn, we just met and you're already trying to get rid of me," he said.

"I don't even know your name," I said.

"I'm Domonique."

On our way to my class we stopped to talk to one of his little girl-friends and she turns to me and says, "Hey, you his new girlfriend?" I didn't know how to answer that because we literally just met, but I also didn't want to get into a fight on the first day of school.

"No, I'm new and he's just helping me get to my class," I said. I won't front. I was a little scared because I thought she was my competition.

"Oh. I don't like him, he's my cousin. Girl, I'm just being nosey," she said.

Domonique laughed at the encounter I had with his cousin and he just walked off. I guess I am in good hands now. His cousin grabbed my schedule and said, "Oh, we are in the same class. You can just walk with me!" I was on a roll and school had just started. I met a boy *and* made a new friend.

"My name is Jaz," she said. "We better hurry up before the bell rings."

"I'm Porcia, thanks again for helping me out."

When we got to class Jaz walked to a row of desks and there was another girl sitting there.

Jaz sat down and introduced me to Sam. "This is Dominique's new girlfriend," she said.

"Hey Sam, it's nice to meet you and I am NOT his girlfriend," I said. "He is cute, tho."

They both gave each other a look then laughed.

In walks the teacher and I couldn't concentrate on anything other than the fact that my antisocial ass just made two friends and a possible new boo in less than five minutes. This is going to be a good year.

Lunch was always my favorite part of the day. Not only do I love to eat, but there was always something happening at our table. On this day, lunch was about to end and this short guy walked up to the table. "You the new girl, huh," he asked me. "Why does everybody keep saying that," I thought to myself.

Aren't we all new here? But because I was new to the district I didn't know a single person. All of them had been going to school with each other since they were in elementary. So no matter how much I tried to fight it, I stood out.

"Yes, I'm new. I'm Porcia," I said.

"I'm J. You need to know who I am," he said.

When lunch was over It was time to head to my last class for the day which was some type of math class. I was horrible in math so this should be fun.

I walked into class and J was standing at the teacher's desk talking to him about something. I made my way to the back of the class to find a seat so I could be invisible for the whole year. I was blind as a bat but I would rather squint from the back of the classroom and mess up my vision than sit up front and get called on to answer a question I didn't know the answer to.

"Why are you sitting in the back," J asked as he walked up to my desk.

"Because I want to. Shouldn't you be looking for a seat too?"

"I'm sitting up front so I can learn something."

The class couldn't go fast enough, I was lost the whole time. J stuck his hand up every chance he got and he spoke so well. He was so smart. Paying attention was the smart thing to do, but I was daydreaming. On my first day of school I met a "bad boy" who skipped class all the time, a guy who was charming and smart, and I made two friends who happened to be cousins of the bad boy. The bell snapped me out of my daydream and it was finally time to go home.

I wasn't going to tell anyone about my day at school because I knew my parents and their questions came with more questions. Once I made it home my dad asked us if we wanted to go to my brother's football practice. I hated football, but I was down for the ride.

Football season is a big deal in Texas and although this was pee wee football, everybody from school was at this practice. Parents had noisemakers and the dads were lined up on the field attempting to coach the coaches. And this was just practice, I couldn't imagine what a game would be like!

I found a spot against the fence while my dad went to get David settled in. Dominique walked up to me and smiled. "What are you doing here," I asked. "My cousin is on this team," he said. I looked around to see where my dad was because I didn't know If I was even allowed to talk to boys, but before I could even open my mouth to say anything, my dad walked up behind us.

"What's your name," he asked Dominique.

"Daddy, this is…"

"The boy can't talk?"

"My name is Dominique, sir," he said with a shaky voice.

"I guess y'all call yourselves liking each other?" He looked at both of us.

How the hell did he come to that conclusion by us just standing here??? I wish the earth could've just swallowed me up at that very moment. I damn sure wasn't quick with words and from the way he charmed me at school today, I assumed he had this one in the bag.

I was wrong.

"We met at school and we are just friends, sir."

"Oh, I like 'just friends'," my dad said. "You just want her draws, don't you?"

"Well, yes sir, but…"

Wait, pause. Did this boy just admit to my dad that he wanted to have sex with me?! How long was this football practice anyway? I was ready to GO. I know my dad was just being a dad, but what a way to knock all the wind out of me without laying a finger on me.

"No, that's not the only reason," Dominique quickly added after realizing what he had said.

"It's too late now. The truth is out," my dad said with the biggest grin on his face. He had successfully sabotaged my first little puppy love interest and he thought I should've been thankful for it. He exposed the big bad 8th grade boy who wanted to have sex with his daughter. But DUH!!! I already knew that's what he wanted. I just liked the fact that I had something to look forward to everyday at school. We were both so embarrassed. I was looking at Dominique thinking, "Really?? What happened to all that charm I saw at school? What were you thinking about?" I was so annoyed.

Football practice was over and it couldn't have come at a better time.

After that day, I breezed through middle school with no major issues. After seeing Dominique with different girls every week and noticing that he was skipping school a lot, I quickly lost interest. I still had to see him sometimes though because Jaz and Sam invited me to all of their family reunions and family functions. We never had anything going on but he always gave me that, "I see you looking good girl," stare and I would melt inside, but I knew better.

It was the summer before we would all be going to high school and I didn't know how to feel about middle school ending. Summer time for me meant going to Hillsboro to visit my mom. I would miss my friends here, but my dad and bonus mom were strict and didn't let me hang out with everyone. So going to Hillsboro was better than sitting in the house.

"Come back home the way you left," my dad said as we pulled into the country.

I hated when he said that because I had no idea what it meant.

"What does that even mean, daddy?"

"It means I'm dropping you off as a virgin, so come back home the same way." He didn't have to worry about me doing anything yet, because I wasn't ready to. Nobody could pressure me into doing anything I didn't want to do, but I never explained that to him. I would just smile and agree.

He already knew the vibes when I went to visit Hillsboro. My mama and Aunt Princess lived in the same apartment complex right next door to each other and they weren't as strict as he and my bonus mom were. I think it's just that country life. My cousins and I were allowed to walk around town, walk to the store, walk to get food…I mean there was just so much freedom!

When we pulled up to my mom's apartment, Nerra was standing outside waiting for me to get out of the car.

"Girl, what are you wearing tonight," she asked me.

"Um, where are we going?"

"Babyyyyyyyy, you know what we do down here. Get you a outfit together!"

We both burst out laughing because she was so serious. The country life is something you have to experience to understand it. Every day was an event.

"Let's go get Tonya and Rae so they can help us pick out an outfit," I said. Tonya and Rae are my first cousins on my mom's side. I had some cute new clothes I wanted to show Tonya anyway.

"Aw hell, my baby is in town." My Aunt Princess was a vibe. We walked in the house, we hugged and asked where the girls were.

"You know they are upstairs finding clothes," she said. "Y'all ain't bout to be hanging out all night either, while y'all up there picking out a full wardrobe." I shot up the stairs to the girls' room and they already had the music blasting and clothes laid out.

We had shit to do. And by shit to do, I mean everybody would pick out an outfit just to sit outside on the porch. This was a process, it was a must that we had our clothes laid out before the sun went down. It was summer time so shorts were the only option. Once we had all showered, oiled up, threw our hair up in a ponytail, and made sure our lips were extra shiny, we danced. If we weren't making up routines to Destiny's Child *Bills Bills Bills*, we were fully shaking our asses to Juvenile's *Back That Ass Up*.

Tonya is the oldest of our crew. She was always so organized and she kept us in check. She was sitting on the floor ironing all of her clothes for the week. "Cuz you need your clothes ironed," she asked me. I told her, "I would love a hug first." She jumped up and we hugged for a long time. We have a bond that can't be explained and she knew I felt free when I was with them.

Tonya started to tell me about this party that she was getting ready for and how she didn't want the other girls to go. Under any other circumstance she probably would've wanted to go alone, but I hadn't spent much time with her so she convinced Aunt Princess to let me tag along. I had no sense of style, had NEVER danced at a party before, and I was sure my parents would never approve of me going, but still, I knew this was a party I couldn't miss.

Uncle Joe would be dropping us off, but first we stopped at this corner house. Tonya motioned for me to get out with her so I could come in and speak and she could let her friends know I would be coming with them. Her friend Mary was the first person to say something to me. "Girl, you're too young to be going with us," she said jokingly. I just smiled because I was just happy to be out with older people. Unc dropped us off at this big white building and told us to be careful. No long lecture, just have fun.

Now Tonya isn't that much older than me, so I was shocked when we walked into the party. All the girls were bent over while all the dudes held up the wall. "You good, cuz," Tonya asked me. I motioned for her to go dance with her friends while I found the nearest corner to tuck away into. I was having fun, but taking it all in at the same time. With each song that played all you could hear through the whole room was, "Ayyyyeee!" The lights were dim and it was scorching hot, but nobody seemed to care. I just kind of bobbed my head and sang the songs I was familiar with, until I heard Juvenile come on. I didn't have a care in the world after that. The rest of the night I was right in the middle of the dance floor sweating with the rest of the crowd. My first "house" party was a success in my eyes. I knew I couldn't tell my parents about the party because I honestly didn't know how they would react to it, but none of that mattered then. I had the time of my life. This is what summertime was like in Hillsboro for me. Every night there was something happening.

It was a Sunday night when my dad and bonus mom came to get me. Summer was over and leaving Hillsboro was *always* bittersweet for me. My dad could always sense that something was off when I got back home, but he never really talked to me about why I was so down after my visits. He would just say, "Every time you come home we have to reprogram you." I'm not a robot so I hated when he told me that. I knew something was missing, but I didn't know how to explain what was happening to me. I was housed, clothed, and fed, which should have been enough. As long as I wasn't having sex everything was "fine" in their eyes. But something was missing for me.

Chapter 3

CITY SLICKER

My dad's house was strict as it related to hanging out. Don't get me wrong, I loved having my own room and all the love in my dad's house, but I certainly missed the freedom I had when I was in the country.

"Porcia D, are you ready to go back-to-school shopping?" My bonus mom walked into my room smiling from ear to ear.

"School doesn't start for another month," I said.

"Yeah, but we want to get ahead of everyone. Besides, shopping is fun."

My bonus mom always showered me with the same love as Tia and David. So I didn't feel like the ugly stepchild. Hell, sometimes she would sneak me away and do things *without* them. I was loved.

Our shopping trips always went the same way. If we say we are going shopping for jeans, then I'm headed straight to one store and hope they have what I like in there. I would follow my bonus mom from section to section and she would hold clothes up and say, "Oh, this will be cute on you." My reply would be, "Yes, ma'am." When I was all the way over it I would respond like my dad when she held him at the mall too long, "Yep, that's cute, let's get two of em." By the time we got to the register she actually had me a complete high school wardrobe put together. At that point I was just ready to go.

There was this guy that lived down the street from us and he and my brother had become friends over the summer. He was kind of cute, but I knew he was trouble. All the cute boys seemed to be trouble at our age. He was cool and he talked to me on the bus ride to school so I wouldn't look like the lonely nerd. I think people mistook my quietness for shyness and for some reason they had to play the, "let's rescue the quiet girl," game. But the reality was, I just didn't feel like doing all that extra talking. I'm a true introvert and small talk is just not my thing so I would just sit and observe everybody and listen to them talk. Half the time they were lying about something and everyone knew it.

This guy was a sophomore so he was giving me the rundown, who to talk to and who to stay away from. I was like, "boy, I have a handful of friends and I am not interested in anyone right now."

The first day of high school was a production for me. There were so many people. So many black people at that. I knew from the moment I stepped foot into that school that it was about to be an interesting ride. Lunch felt like the cafeteria scene from the movie *Save the Last Dance*. Some people, the normal ones, sat down to eat lunch while others sat *on* the tables. The table across from me was full of dudes making beats with their pencils and freestyling to whatever beat they made. It was a whole thing. I sat with Jaz and Sam for the most part and they had a bunch of friends. My freshman year was when I met Ebony and Sarah. I know you're thinking, "good job Porcia, you are on a roll with this whole friend thing." Yeah well, I was not. I barely talked around the people I wasn't close to. Ebony and Sarah were mutual friends of Jaz and Sam so we just naturally meshed. Ebony and I would eventually end up on the track team together, so we ran during the spring and summer.

By this time J and I were best friends. He was already very close to Jaz and Sam, so our friendships just worked out. He was an athlete and every girl, white *and* black, stayed in his face. One day in school, we hugged and in true J fashion he started joking with everybody we walked by. A tall skinny white girl came sashaying through the hall and walked right up to us. "Hey, J," she said in the most annoying voice ever. I didn't have anything against any of J's Flavors of the Week, but she was the true definition of a culture vulture, but still, I wasn't rude to her. I told J I would holler at him at lunch and I set off to find Jaz and Sam. J had these girls wrapped around his finger. He had them on a schedule too, they all knew their place and were fine with that.

As soon as I hit the corner I saw Dominique whispering in some girl's ear. "What's good?" I said as I kept making my way up the stairs. "Hey, P. How was your summer?"

"It was decent, I went to visit my mom so that was nice. I'll catch up with you later," I said.

I laughed to myself because hanging with his girl cousins allowed me to get all the scoop on him, so I was far from interested. Okay, I'm lying, I still melted on the inside every time I saw him, but I held it together.

Before long, the first part of 9th grade was down and Christmas break was approaching, which meant that it was time to head back to visit my mom.

I called Tonya up to see when her school went on break. "Hey boo, what's going on? You are in high school now so it's parties here all break long. What time is Uncle D bringing you down?" She asked. I didn't want to bug my dad so I just told her, "girl, you know how that goes." We both laughed. My daddy hated for me to go to the country so it felt like he took his precious time taking me.

"Well alright, I can't wait until you get down here. I have so much to tell you."

I always knew when we made it to Hillsboro. I fell asleep every single car ride, but I would wake up to the feeling of bumps in the road. There were these strips on the road that made a rhythmic cadence when you drove over them. Once I heard that specific noise, I knew we were officially in the country.

The courthouse downtown had the same Christmas decorations every year. As we made our way deeper into town there were snowflakes and wreaths on each stop light and the local businesses had their window displays up.

My mom and parents chatted for a couple of minutes and then, the country was mine for the next week. The sun started to go down and a few people started to trickle out of their apartments. Me and Rae were on the porch cracking up. She was good at impersonating people. She started talking like this boy we knew and I died laughing. I heard somebody a few feet down laugh real loud and in true Black people fashion, he had run out in the street. After that little show Dominique put on for my daddy, I was pretty much over the fact that I would like anybody else. Until tonight. I was drawn to this boy.

Either he didn't usually come to the apartments or I just never paid any attention to him, but this night he stood out. Every time he opened his mouth everybody was amused and his laugh was really distinct. I asked Rae who he was and she said, "Oh, that's Fatz. Him and Tonya are in the same grade."

"Oh." I said.

"You like him, don't you?" It seemed like she screamed at the top of her lungs.

"He's just funny," I responded. "Every time he says something everybody laughs hard as hell."

I got quiet for a minute, then I got bold. I told her to go tell him I said what's up. What the hell did I mean? What's up? What's up with what? Did you think of what to say if he said, "what's up with what," dummy? I hadn't thought about that. I just knew it was something about him.

"Fatz!" Rae said out freaking loud. She burst out laughing and said, "naw I'm playing." She went over there and it was literally like a scene out of one of those cheesy high school movies. He turned around, looked at me, smiled, then charmed the hell out of me. We didn't talk that night, but he told Rae to tell me, "Shid, what's up with it?" And left it at that. After that we just kind of gave each other the eye the whole night. He made sure to direct his jokes my way so that I could crack a smile. Hell, I was full out laughing, there was no need to be shy now. I was smitten.

Since Tonya was the oldest, Aunt Princess let me go with her when she walked to her friend's house on the other side of town. I asked her what type of guy Fatz was and before I finished saying his name she said, "speaking of Fatz, he is right there." He was walking right in our direction. I didn't notice this the other night, but he was really tall. His hair was braided to the back, he was dressed unlike anyone I had seen in town, and he had that same charming smile from when we saw each other the first time.

When Fatz and I locked eyes we just kept walking towards each other and we gave each other the warmest hug. He smelled so good. It shocked me because I didn't know him like that, but I was showing OUT.

"What's your real name?" I asked him. He paused and looked at me for a second. "Everybody calls me Fatz."

"I'm not everybody," I said looking into his eyes.

"Wade," he said with that smirk.

"That's what I'll be calling you," I told him with more sass than I knew I had. I was showing out in the country!

Wade and I instantly connected with each other and I knew that that would make it harder for me to leave town. I wouldn't tell my dad and bonus mom about him because I didn't know how that conversation, better yet, that lecture, would go. What I did know was that they said I could date at 16, and I would be 16 in the summer, so technically it was fine. Normally I would split the holidays up between my parents, but after meeting Wade, I wanted to spend every holiday in Hillsboro. Every free minute I had I was planning on how I was going to get to Hillsboro.

Summertime had come back around after my sophomore year in high school and Wade and I were in a full on long distance relationship. I still hadn't told my parents about him because I knew deep down he wasn't the ideal guy they would want me with, but the connection was deep. We would talk on the phone and when we couldn't reach each other I would have Tonya pass messages for me. It didn't matter what he was doing or what time I made it to Hillsboro, he would be at my mama's house within 15 minutes. He would get out of the car talking shit, but in a charming way. He would say something about my pigeon toes and bow legs. "What's good, Black," he said as he picked me up off my feet. I was in love.

The first 30 minutes in town hit me differently now that Wade and I were a couple. We would sit in each other's face and talk. If the weather was nice we would walk for hours and talk about everything. He didn't care about anything but me. He didn't care that my parents were becoming famous, he didn't care about any flaws I had. We just clicked. He knew I was a virgin and in the beginning he was down with respecting it, but he was also a 17-year-old boy. I knew the deal but still, none of that mattered when we were together. I made it very clear that I had love for him, but that I was not ready to have sex and he respected me. I always knew that I would do things my way. When I wanted to start having sex I was going to. I can't name one time where I felt pressured. He had become my best friend.

Our first real date was to his mom's wedding, which is a hell of a first date. I had packed this really pretty blue dress with some wedge heels so I knew what my outfit would be once I got down there. He called my mama's house phone and told me he would be there to pick me up in 30 minutes. I felt so special. Like, "Oh, he drives and I'm riding with him." I was only 16, but in my mind, we were so going to get married.

I loved the fact that he paid attention to me. He noticed when I changed my hair, he noticed if I had new clothes, he was just in tune. After meeting his family I started to go everywhere with him. My mama trusted me and she liked him so she was cool with me hanging out with him. I just had to be back to her house by the end of the night. The last day I was in town was reserved for quality time between us.

"I wish you would talk your pops into letting you live down here."

"Boy, you know damn well my daddy ain't going for that. He knows what goes on in these small towns."

"He wants you to be a city slicker all ya life, huh," he said with the cutest smirk on his face.

After that, we just got lost in each other. Two kids standing in the middle of the street with not a care in the world.

We started to walk back towards my mama's house and as we made our way around the corner I heard a girl's voice.

"Niggas these days," she shouted and everyone started laughing.

I was so confused. First of all, who the hell was yelling in the middle of the night and who was she talking to? I turned to Wade and asked him if he knew any of them. He paused and I gave him a look. We don't lie to each other. Well at least, I didn't lie to him.

"I used to talk to the girl in the white shirt before I met you. She's mad because I'm with you now."

"Well, she better keep that shit on her porch. It ain't my fault I scooped you up."

We laughed hard as hell as we walked off. We made it back to my mama's house and it was too late for him to come inside. We kissed a thousand times and said our goodbyes.

"You better go straight home." I told him.

"You already know what it is, Black. I'm going home to wait for you to call me."

Damn, I loved this boy.

Nerra was inside on the phone. "Girl, where you and Fatz been?" She asked.

"You know we be trying to get that last minute time in. Summer is almost over for me and I'm going to miss him."

"You know they said him and KK was messing around. I know you really like him, but be careful. Ima make sure I keep my eye on him for you because you can't trust these boys down here."

"Thanks, sis. And who the hell is KK?"

"Girl, she kin to a bunch of people down here. I'll have to ask Tonya what they be doing at school for you."

"Don't spy on him." I said.

All of a sudden, I remembered something. "I forgot to give him his necklace back. See if your friend will drive us to his mama's house," I said.

"Girl, y'all *just* left each other. You just trying to go see that boy again. Talking about a damn necklace," she said laughing.

"Just ask her for a ride, lil girl."

We hit a few blocks before we turned down his street. I saw a few people standing in the street in front of his house and I was thinking, "Oh good, he's outside so I don't have to go in." As I got closer, the car slowed down and I saw him standing by a car drinking something, and there was a girl standing extra close to him. So much for waiting on me to call you. I rolled the window down and we locked eyes. He knew he had messed up. I tossed the necklace to him, rolled up the window, and me and Nerra pulled off. Everything I felt was still there, but just like that, the relationship was now tainted. I no longer trusted him.

I thought long and hard on the ride back to my parents. I had so much to tell J when I made it back to the city. I thought Wade and I were better than this. Eventually I drifted off to sleep and by the time I woke up we were pulling into our driveway. I bolted straight up the stairs and flopped on my bed. How could he do this to me? I know I wasn't giving up the goodies, but damn. Is what we have really not that special? Was that the KK girl? I had so many thoughts running through my head with no one to talk to.

Once one girl was in the picture you can bet 4 or 5 more popped up. Wade was my heart, but I hated Fatz. Fatz was a player in every sense of the word. One night Nerra took me over to one of her friend's houses before going out. We stepped into her friend's room and I sat on the bed. I looked around the room and I noticed a mirror that had a bunch of names written in permanent marker. At the very top of the mirror in bold letters I saw F-A-T-Z. It was odd to me, but not surprising. How many more girls had he charmed? My immature mindset couldn't help but think that if I lived in the same town as him all of this would stop. I knew it was time for me to back away from him. All of a sudden, my trips to Hillsboro were not as exciting for me anymore.

Another school year rolled around and The school district drew a big red line through the city and the schools were split. Most of the people I ran track with stayed at the original campus but because of my family's address, I moved to the new Mansfield High School. By my junior year in high school I had come all the way out of my shell. I was on the track team and I was pretty good. The middle school body I had was no more and I was all legs. I didn't have too much booty, but I was fine.

We had two "babysitters" during the time my parents had to travel. We were old enough to look after ourselves, but my parents would be gone for months at a time all over the world. So we needed someone at home with us. My granny Sandra moved into our house to help my parents out with us, but eventually that changed. One weekend when I went to visit Hillsboro she snapped at Tia and David. I don't know how the conversation went between my parents and Granny Sandra, but that weekend was enough to make my parents reevaluate some things and My bonus mom's sister, Aunt Duke, eventually came in and she was with us for a while. Aunt Duke wasn't strict at all. She allowed me to be a teen. My parents ran a tight ship so I didn't ask to go to many places. I went to a couple of step shows, but my curfew was early. By the time my friends were headed to any type of after party it was time for me to be home. The only time I went to anything is when I would spend the night over Jaz or Sam's house. Their parents allowed them more freedom than I had so I knew that was my way into creating memories with them. Since I was limited on what I could participate in, I would spend my weekends in the house watching classic movies with Aunt Duke. *The Players Club* was in heavy rotation. We quoted every line of that movie every time we watched it.

J and I had gotten to the point where we hung out more often. I would go to his house on the weekends and chill over there the whole day. His mom was a police officer so she worked a lot, but when she was off I would eat dinner at their home with them. Ms. Pajji had such a sweet spirit, but she didn't play. She had two boys in her home and their house was spotless. J also knew how to cook and he was always doing something around their house. I silently admired his mom because of her strength and the values she instilled in her boys.

The years of athletics had started to show on J. His body was a masterpiece so I was very attracted to him. He was one of my best friends and he understood me. If I had a crush on someone he was the first person to know about it. He didn't have an exclusive girlfriend, but I knew about his flavors of the week. I didn't care much about that because I was cool with what we had going on. No politics, no titles, just super close. Although J was a ladies' man, I knew he was going to be mine one day. I was still a virgin and up until this point I never wanted to be with anyone sexually, but my thoughts were beginning to change.

Peer pressure was the determining factor for sex for most people my age, but I always knew that my first time having sex would be my decision. I didn't want to start having sex just because people at school were talking about it. What might have been cool for them may have put me in a bad situation. It had to happen when I was ready, and I was starting to feel like I was ready. Aside from the physical things that started to happen to my body, I was emotionally connected to J, but we had never been intimate. I wanted the first time to be in my bed. The only thing about that was that my bed was still in my parents' house; I had to figure out a day they would be gone.

The day came. Not only would my parents be out of the house, Tia and David were going somewhere too. The details of this day were a blur for me at the beginning. I remember everyone leaving, I don't even remember why J came to the house that day. That's how much we frequented each other's homes. I remember getting on the phone with Tonya to ask her what she thought about losing your virginity. Before I could get anything out, I heard Nerra in the background asking to speak to me.

"Girl, Fatz and that white girl had a baby together," she said.

My heart skipped a few beats. Wade and I had grown apart for a number of reasons. I was never under the impression that I was his only person. The puppy love we shared was deep but I wasn't naive. So many things had happened between us that tainted the trust. Although I knew he had other things going on, he always gave me the attention I thought I needed.

One weekend, after things had ended between us, I went to visit Hillsboro and Wade and I linked up. He knew I was in a relationship with J so he poured it on extra heavy. He couldn't keep his hands to himself and I melted right into it. We kissed the night before I left that weekend and all I could think was that I had to tell J. That kiss with Wade crushed J.

Tonya and I hung up and I waited for J to come over. I couldn't let what I just heard about Wade affect me. I was in love with J and was considering giving him my most prized possession. I needed to focus. I loved Wade, but not like I loved J.

I lost my virginity that day and most of the details I have to keep for myself. I have never shared some of my firsts with anyone because they are sacred to me. Our souls most definitely tied that day and I fell deeper. After the first time I was addicted. Our senior year was bliss. I would skip class and go to J's house. I had officially become a woman and I needed J all the time. My life felt like it was going the way I wanted it to. I didn't need anything or anyone else. We were about to graduate high school together and for me, soon enough, our forever after would start.

After graduation and all of the graduation parties there was one last senior thing to do. My senior class had well over 500 people, but only 7 of us signed up to go to Cancun for our senior class trip. J and I linked up to convince his mom and my parents to let us go. I had almost $800 from my graduation party, plus my parents gave me a little extra. I was really surprised that my parents agreed that I could go because I didn't even get to go away much in town. I didn't complain at all though. It was my senior year and I was grateful. The night before we left, J and I talked about all the things we would do there. I had never had a drink, but it was legal for people our age to drink there. He popped my cherry already so sex on the beach went to the top of the list. I was in love. I could hardly sleep the night before we left because I was thinking about all the things I wanted to do. I finally drifted off because our flight was an early one.

The plane was full of horny hyper seniors. I had never been on a trip like this, especially unsupervised. When we touched down in Cancun we had to ride in this shaky minivan to get to our resort. Once we checked in with the trip chaperones, the girls in our group had already made a plan to hit up the local Walmart to buy drink mixers. J had really bad motion sickness so when we stopped by one of the local stores I got him some food because we hadn't eaten yet. He laid on my lap when I came out of the store, then I told him I got him some snacks. He gave me this look like, "I didn't ask you for all of that, but you looking out for me. I appreciate that." All I got was a couple of Gatorades and some unhealthy snacks, but I think this was one of those, "you thought about me," moments. He was my boyfriend and I didn't want him to pass out on our first day in Mexico.

I went to school with predominantly white people and most of them had been drinking since we were freshmen in high school. They knew exactly what to get to mix the drinks and everything. I was just there taking it all in. Apparently, there is something exciting about getting new people wasted because they couldn't wait to get me drunk.

We checked into our rooms, changed out of our travel clothes, then we headed to paint the town. Our first stop was a place called Senor Frogs. Tacos and beer is what was on the menu for our table. My first beer was my last because what the hell. One of the girls handed me a corona and I got a mouth full of bubbles. The taste made me gag and I knew EARLY that beer wasn't for me. I'll just take some tacos.

Once we got to the first club, I asked J to get me something to drink. He came back over to us with a cup full of brown liquor. When I tasted it, all I could taste was Coca Cola quickly followed by Crown or Hennessy. I wasn't a drinker but I knew what he drank. "They didn't have any fruity drinks over there," I asked.

"You will be fine, I got you," he said. "Enjoy yourself, we are in Cancun."

Say less. The DJ got on the microphone and announced a dance contest and guess who was one of the first people standing on the bar with my white girl friends dancing? Yours truly.

I had on a pink mini skirt and I had to show the people who I was. Hillsboro came out that night. The more dancing I did the drunker I felt. I told J we needed to go because I started to feel bad. I talked shit to everybody on our way to catch the shuttle and when we got on the shuttle I tried to fight this guy AND his girlfriend. It was safe to say that I wasn't a fun drunk. J grabbed me by the shoulders and told me to chill before he went to jail out there. I don't remember anything else from that night.

The next day the girls and I came up with a plan to invite some guys who were there from another school into our room. I knew better. I was black, we did not play that, but there I was in the mix. I didn't have any intentions on doing anything with either of the guys, but I was on my senior trip. I knew I definitely wanted to make the best of it, so if that meant kicking it with new guys then I was down. We told them to come back later, but to call first so we could make sure J and the other guys were not in our room. There were only two of us that came on this trip with our boyfriends so we had to tread lightly. I was having so much fun being free that I didn't even realize the fact that I was disrespecting J. It turns out that I have the worst luck; J and the guys came down to our room to see if we wanted to go get tattoos that night. I really wanted a tattoo, but I couldn't slide a tattoo past my parents. That was a battle I did not want to fight. The guys made themselves comfortable in our room as we continued to talk about the plans for the night. We were all giving each other the eye, and I had knots in my stomach hoping the guys we invited over didn't call. The hotel phone rang loud. When J picked it up I knew we were caught.

Before he slammed the phone down he yelled something in Spanish to the guy on the other end. I had no idea what he said so, against my better judgment, I asked what it meant. He barely even looked up at me. He knew we were up to something. On his way out the door he picked up a glass and shattered it. I sat on the bed thinking to myself, "I have officially ruined our senior trip."

After we got dressed I went to J's room and spent the next couple of hours trying to convince him that I didn't care about anybody but him. I didn't have a desire to do anything with either one of those guys, I was really just being hot in the ass as my grandmother called it. We broke away from the group to get ourselves together, then we made our way to the nearest tattoo shop. I knew that I was way too afraid of what my parents would say to get a tattoo, so I decided to get my bellybutton pierced instead. J ended up getting a superman tattoo on his chest and I remember being so nervous for him. I could easily slip a navel ring out to hide it from my parents, but you can't hide a tattoo. The next day the chaperones asked us to take a group photo to show our parents. I knew that I had to either stand behind someone or put my hand over my belly button because if my parents saw my stomach they were going to flip. They were NOT the ones to pull this on.

Our time in Cancun was coming to an end, but J and I still had a couple of things we wanted to do. I got drunk for the first time and J and I had our first major vacation argument, but we hadn't had sex on the beach yet.

It turns out that sex on the beach is not as sexy as it sounds. The moment started out really cute. We took a walk, held hands, and took a moment to just be boyfriend and girlfriend. Once we knew we were completely alone we knew what needed to be done. Beach sex is hyped up way too much. There was sand everywhere, which instantly killed the mood. Having sand get into your lady areas is a very uncomfortable feeling. We didn't have a blanket with us so we lay bare back on the sand trying to make love. We laughed so hard because we just knew it was about to be like the movies. Instead, it was an epic fail, but at least sex on the beach was checked off the list and we weren't arguing anymore.

Mexico was monumental for our relationship. There were firsts I shared with him that will forever be etched in my heart.

There was one thing on my calendar that I missed while I was having a wild time in Mexico. I forgot to call my bonus mom on her birthday. Not only did I forget to call her, but it hadn't dawned on me until I had to call her to make sure she would be picking us up from the airport. Before we got on the plane we talked to J's mom and told her how much fun we had. She wasn't super strict so we gave her more details than I planned on giving my own parents. And this is where I messed up. I forgot to ask her not to mention every detail to my bonus mom when she and my mom spoke later. Big mistake. Before the plane landed my parents knew about me drinking on top of the fact that I had missed my bonus mom's birthday. The car ride was bound to be a long, awkward one. As soon as I got in the car I felt the tension. She was mad. "My friends didn't give you that money at your graduation for you to go out and buy alcohol," she said. If she was this mad about me drinking then I know the belly ring would send her over the edge. I slid closer to the door and put my purse in my lap. I slipped my hand under my shirt to unscrew the ring and pulled it out of my stomach. All I could think about was the fact that I would have to go through the pain of having it pierced again. I knew I would get it repierced when I turned 18 in a month or so.

Turning 18 was a big deal. High school was over and it was time to step into the real world. I had no clue what I wanted to do with my life so I applied to community college to keep my parents off my back.

I could no longer live in their house and not have anything going on. I didn't have an issue with going to school, but I was just wandering around blindly. I was taking classes, but I didn't know where I wanted to end up. My mother went to college and got her degree and my parents only knew the entertainment industry. Where in the world did I fit in? I didn't know if I wanted to pursue a career in the same industry as my parents or follow in my mom's footsteps and go to college. All of them were successful in their own ways, but what did Porcia want to do?

J would be going off to college soon and I was just stuck. He would always encourage me to try new things to help spark something in me, but it didn't always work. We always knew he was going to be this intellectual being that had college figured out before he even graduated, but I played around most of the time he spent applying to schools. I knew I had to figure my life out, but it was difficult for me. I didn't know my purpose in life so I started to do anything and everything.

J and I were still going strong in our relationship, but I felt like I was holding him back. We were young and in love so we did everything to stay together. Our families spent holidays and birthdays together. One year my parents planned a huge Christmas party and invited everyone we knew. It did not alarm me because this was something that happened often. They told me I could invite my mom and Nerra. They also invited J's family and a million other people. The guest list maxed out at about 250. I was confused about a lot of things in my life at that time, but one thing was clear to me, I was loved. J had his ways but he was truly my best friend. We built a friendship for years before we started dating. We were in tune. But on this night, he kept disappearing and I didn't understand where he was going. There were a lot of our family and friends there, but we normally were in each other's faces at every function. Everyone gathered in the formal living area because my dad had an announcement to make. He thanked everyone for coming out to celebrate with them and he started a game. J was holding a teddy bear which I thought was odd. I did get a little nervous because all of the attention was on us. J was extra so I knew something was about to happen, but I didn't expect to see him down on one knee. Time stood still for a minute. I looked up to see my dad smiling from ear to ear. Everyone else in the room was a blur and moved in slow motion. I shifted my focus back down to J. "You're my best friend and I want to spend the rest of my life with you," he said. I didn't hesitate to say yes. He was my best friend. He was my introduction to every type of intimacy, so I was honored actually.

Eventually I realized that being engaged wasn't the best idea for me. I had no idea what it entailed to be someone's wife. Being a wife is more than just keeping the house and having the babies. You truly have to die to yourself and consider someone else for the rest of your time together. I didn't fully understand the sacrifice and commitment of it all. This next confession may come as a shock, but my communication was horrible, and I had no intention to improve in any of those areas in my life.

I loved J, but life was tugging me in a different direction. I started getting attention from other men and I ate it up. I thought it was cute and I started entertaining these dudes. I ended up cheating on J with someone who wasn't worth it and I hated myself for it for a long time. Still though, I kept doing it and J took me back time after time. I was low down for the way I treated him. After a while, he told me that I couldn't keep hurting him in that way and he decided to take the engagement ring back. I wasn't ready to be what he needed me to be at the time so we went our separate ways. We stayed in touch through the years, but the relationship would never be the same. I had done way too much damage.

Chapter 4

WADE AND MADDY

WADE and I had that, "pick up where we left off," chemistry. We didn't have to rekindle anything because the flame never went out. We always kept in touch and once me and J broke up, Wade and I started hanging out again. The only difference this time was that we were really grown. We could explore each other on a physical level now, and I was all in. My parents and I were arguing more because I was going to Hillsboro to visit him frequently. I was working for them at the time as their assistant and I wasn't taking the job seriously anymore.

One Friday I was going to go visit him and my dad asked me to finish my work before I left. I didn't finish the work, I just left and went to Hillsboro because I was ready to see Wade. I was supposed to return back to work the following Monday, but my car broke down that weekend. My radiator had a huge hole in it. There was no way I could ask my parents to help me get my car fixed, they were already mad about me driving to Hillsboro so much in the first place. I decided to call my dad to tell him what was going on and that I didn't think I would make it back to work on Monday because I needed to get the car fixed.

Monday came around and the shade tree mechanic that I found to work on the car told me he needed at least a week to fix it. Although I knew I needed to get back home and back to work, all I could think about was the fact that I get to spend more time with Wade. I didn't care about going back to my parents' house at that point. Life in the country with my new boyfriend seemed like the best idea at 20 years old.

A week went by and I didn't even call into work or call my parents. I wanted to just show up with the car fixed on my own so they didn't have anything to say. When we finally did speak, I could hear the anger and disappointment in my father's voice when he fired me and told me that I had to find somewhere else to live because I wasn't performing the duties that I was supposed to for my job. I could have easily gone back home and made amends with my parents, but I was in love...

A few weeks went by before I went back to my dad's house and moved all of my things to Hillsboro with my mom and Nerra. We were finally back together and my mother was the happiest I had seen her in a long time. She promised to help me get where I needed to be and assured me that life isn't over because of what happened between my parents and I. She constantly reminded me that I am the daughter of a King and I should think like that no matter the circumstances. She was absolutely right. Once all of my things were settled into the apartment, we went over the house rules. I didn't care what the rules were. I would follow every single one of them as long as I got to see Wade every day. The plan was for me to live with my mother until I found a job and my own apartment. Although this town held a special place in my heart, its deep-rooted racism would make my job search difficult. In most small towns the "good" paying jobs are occupied by people who have been with the company for years. I really did aim high at the beginning of my search. I started at the courthouse. Here I was, a young Black woman making my way into the same courthouse that once released a man to an angry mob to be lynched. The heinous crime took place years before I was even a thought, but the history still stained this town. I walked through the heavy doors and made my way up the stairs. The stares started instantly. The deeper I got into the building the bolder the questions became: "Ma'am, are you lost?"

"Are you here for court?" I politely asked to be pointed in the direction of the job applications. I took the application and found a bench and got comfortable. I needed a job as soon as possible so I had no time to spare.

Ever optimistic, I sat there and filled out the application. This wasn't an issue because I was a smart girl and a fast learner. I picked up a few skills while working for my parents so this job would be a breeze. There was just one thing, I had to get the job first. A week later I got a call to inform me that the position had been filled, but my application would be kept on file. I already knew what that meant. I needed to keep looking and expand my search if I wanted to see immediate money.

I had put in applications all over town. I went from only applying for desk jobs to applying for fast food and waitressing jobs. I hadn't worked in either field before, but the money I brought to town with me was dwindling down. Wade wasn't working at the time so if I got a job I could sustain both of us. I was a silly young woman and I was in love. There was nothing anyone could have told me to make me change my mind. I finally landed an interview at The Black Eyed Pea, an American restaurant. I didn't eat there often because I only saw elderly people going there. I didn't have anything against them, I just didn't have a taste for that type of food. It reminded me of Lubys. The pay that was offered was $2.13 an hour on top of the tips I got to take home every day. I had never worked as a waitress, but I needed to start making money like yesterday. I knew how to put my words together so getting through the interview phase wasn't a problem for me. I did my good talking to the manager that day and she offered me the job. I quickly reminded her before I left that I was available to start immediately. She chuckled and asked me if I could start training the next day. And just like that I was a waitress. I was a fast learner so my training flew by and I was on the floor within a week.

My time as a waitress opened my heart and my eyes to the realities that a lot of us are facing. Restaurant workers depend on your tips to eat and live. We worked double shifts just to make bill money for the month. I have to admit, I wasn't the greatest tipper before I was hired as a waitress. In past times when I walked into a restaurant I was only there to eat and maybe tip a few dollars. I was now on the other side of the fence and it forced me to respect the hustle.

There are always downsides to everything. I normally try not to focus on those, but sometimes they are too loud to ignore. The restaurant I worked in was in a predominantly white town. Most of the guests that patronized the restaurant were Caucasian, but occasionally we had a Black family that came in. The servers would hover around the host stand whispering and I would be confused about what was happening. "What were they whispering about?" I would go stand next to the host to see what the hush was all about. The host turned to me and asked if I wanted to take the table that just walked through the door. I looked down at the chart that was sitting on the host stand to see that it wasn't my turn to be serving again. One of the other servers clocked the Black family coming through the door and passed the table off to me. I didn't turn down any money and I knew not to judge a book by its cover, so I accepted it. Black people had a bad reputation when it came to tipping, but the people still needed to be taken care of. I took the table and that family tipped me well. I made it a point to go let the server who had passed on them know. I thought it would've been a lesson to him, but it kept happening. They called them Canadians. All I would hear is, "there's Canadians walking in," and everybody would look to me to wait on the Black guests that came in even if my section was already full. I'm not sure who they thought they were dealing with, but I put a stop to that real quick. If it was my turn then I took the tables, but that's where it stopped. I was no longer willing to accept what they were dishing out and I soon became the unpopular Black girl.

Wade would pick me up after every shift. The tips I started to make were enough to feed both of us every day and keep gas in the car. At that time that was the life I thought I wanted. What I didn't know was that he was living two of them.

I'm not sure if you're familiar with Myspace, but it was my introduction to social media. You were able to create a profile with a background that fit your personality and there was a special VIP section with 8 slots reserved for your boo thang and closest friends.

I was not prepared for what I saw when I went to Wade's daughter's mother's Myspace page. I clicked on her profile and the first thing I noticed was a countdown and next to it said 4 months until the new baby comes. NEW BABY? I picked up the phone and got Wade on the line QUICK.

"What's good, Black," he said, all giddy and shit.

"Who is your baby mama pregnant by?"

"What do you mean?"

"Don't play with me," I said.

"I swear I was going to tell you," he began. "I went to her house to talk about seeing my daughter and we got to talking and reminiscing and ended up having sex. Black, I swear I'm sorry, I love you so much, I don't want to be with her."

I felt sick to my stomach. How could he do this to me? To us. I sat on the phone silently sobbing.

"Black, please say something."

"What the hell do you want me to say?"

"Tell me you'll never leave me."

I felt a flutter in my stomach. You're probably thinking it's butterflies, huh? Hell no. That was stupidity floating around because I started to feel *bad* for wanting to leave him. I moved to town and we were having the time of our lives. We dreamt as kids of living like this. We always wanted to live in the same town, go to the same school, and be able to get to each other when we wanted. How did we get *here*?

The connection was so pure and toxic at the same time and I didn't fully understand what I was getting myself into. Even after learning he was about to have another child with this woman, I still wanted to have a child with him.

Valentine's day was approaching and we made a plan to make a baby together. In my mind this would bring us closer. Before Maddison was even conceived we knew her name. This baby was planned. Now our daughter and their new daughter would be born 4 months apart. Wade and I spent a lot of nights on the back roads of Hillsboro; riding around, vibing, and talking. That was the best form of intimacy for me. A lot of talk about our future and about the way we would raise our daughter, and we would laugh at the fact that we were once just two kids who dreamt about spending this much time with each other and now it was our reality.

During my pregnancy I stayed away from my family. Shame mixed with guilt and judgment didn't make me feel good about myself or anyone for that matter. I had even stopped talking to Jaz and Sam. One weekend Jaz called to invite me up to the city to celebrate her birthday. I was about 5 months pregnant at the time. Her birthday was 2 days before mine and I had no plans to do anything so I decided to go. I didn't know what to wear, I hadn't even told my friends that I was pregnant with my first child. I started overthinking the entire process.

On the night of the party, the warmth and acceptance I received from them was the same thing I felt when I met them in the halls of that middle school. Their love was pure and genuine. J was there also, and with no judgment in his eyes, he rubbed my very pregnant belly and smiled.

"I love you, girl," he said in a crowded club.

That night made me want to get my life together. Seeing my friends flourish in their lives gave me hope.

The first time I went around my family after spending a long time away was for my little brother's graduation. I called my dad to see if Wade could come with me and although he wasn't fond of Wade, he wanted to see my face. I was also pregnant with his child so Wade wasn't going anywhere anytime soon. We watched my brother get his high school diploma then we went to Dave and Busters to celebrate afterwards. My anxiety was on a new level because this was the first time Wade and my father were going to be in the same room together in a really long time. Things could have gone one of two ways. They could get into a bad argument and the day would be ruined or everyone would be on their best behavior.

I am so glad the maturity was there. Everybody got along, we laughed, they cracked jokes, and I realized how much Wade and my brother favored one another. It was actually weird once I came to that realization.

Let's fast forward to the third trimester of my pregnancy.

Wade and I started to drift apart. He started working and when he would get off of work he would come home and get right into the shower and then leave. He wouldn't come back until 2 or 3 in the morning. I was so afraid to be alone so I didn't say anything. When I did ask him where he was going he would say to see my daughter. I knew what that meant. He was still seeing his daughter's mother because there was no real explanation for going to her house late at night. His daughter was probably in bed. One morning his phone rang and it was his mama.

"She is about to have the baby! Get to the hospital!"

His second child was born while his third one had temporarily taken over my body.

There was one particular weekend after the birth of his second child that hurts to even think about. I had gotten so big and I didn't do anything but work and go home. During this pregnancy I gained about 65 pounds and it was all in my ass and hips. Nerra had convinced me that I needed to get out. So I decided to get myself together and have a good time. My party outfit was an oversized shirt with some leggings. Wade was adamant about going out this night too, so I needed to see what was up. I thought he was trying to get out to see another girl, but when we got to the party his *baby mama* was there. I didn't understand why I was even going through this with him. I really was bad as hell. Both of my parents' genes had those soul snatching hips running strong in their DNA. My ass was right and I had a head on my shoulders. I wasn't intimidated by her at all, so I just continued to enjoy myself. Wade walks up to me after a couple of minutes to tell me that she is disrespecting him. "Come slap this girl, Black." In my mind I was like, "sir, I am almost 7 months pregnant."

There had been a lot of drinking going on and she was drunk and showing out. Hell, I don't blame her. I was ready to drop my baby so I could get my body back. By the time I made it over to her, she grabbed me and we started fighting! I hit her and the bouncer scooped me up so high off the ground. By the time I convinced him to put me down I looked up and saw Nerra drag his baby mama's ass all the way out the front door. The party was over for me. This is exactly why I should've stayed my ass at home. They were definitely still messing around, but I couldn't focus on that at that moment. Stress wasn't good for my unborn child.

My mother and Nerra decided to throw me a baby shower. I needed to see my friends and family during this time. Jaz and Sam agreed to come to the shower now that it was in the city and I was ecstatic. We clowned when we were together. They knew Wade because I talked about him so much when we were in school. The baby shower was intimate. Both of my mothers, grandmothers, sisters, cousins, and friends were there. Maddison would be coming into a loving environment. My heart was full after the baby shower.

When I reached the last few weeks of my pregnancy, I pretty much knew that my relationship with Wade was coming to an end. All I kept thinking about was how absurd it is for me to continue being with this boy after all of the things he put me through. I felt so broken and alone and because I had shut all of my family out, I had no-one to go to.

Christmas was approaching and I knew I needed to be at home, to be around my family, and just clear my mind. I will never let anyone ruin the most wonderful time of the year! I called my parents and told them I was coming down for a little while. I packed a few things and headed to the city. The first phone call I made when I came back was to Wade. I heard a female voice in the background and I immediately knew who it was. I asked him what was going on. The words I had been dreading flew out of his mouth with ease.

"I don't want to be with you anymore, I want to make it work with Linda and I have already moved all of my stuff in with her."

My heart was so broken to the point where I begged him not to do this to me. "I am pregnant with your daughter, I love you so much. Please don't do this to me."

What I know now that I didn't know then was that if he could leave her so easily after they had a child together and start a new "relationship" with me, then I could receive the same treatment. I was crazy in love and because of that I was blind. I was so blind that I ignored the signs and all of the red flags.

Wade and I didn't talk much until I went into labor with her. I called him when I was about to go to the hospital and crossed my fingers; we were so disconnected that I didn't even know if he would show up for the birth of our daughter. When I gave birth to Maddison, my entire family was there. I had pain medicine so I didn't feel too much of anything. I was comfortable. In the delivery room with me was my dad and Wade. I didn't ever think I would see this day. This was the first time in my life that I couldn't find the words to express the joy in my heart. Wade for sure dogged me out, but he introduced me to parts of my soul that I didn't know existed. That hurt forced me to grow up, quick.

Nothing prepares you for childbirth. You can read every book ever written and still not be prepared for this emotional ride. When things started to speed up, the nurses started to break down the bed and the doctor was paged over the loudspeaker.

I started to feel nauseous and light headed, then the nauseous feeling started to fade and I felt like I had to go to the restroom. The epidural held the pain back, but the pressure I felt down below was massive. The nurse tells me, "Ok, grab both of your legs and bare down until I tell you to push."

I started to push, and although there was not much pain, I felt my daughter making her way into this crazy world. "How would this change me? What type of mother would I be?" All of these questions would have to be answered through experience because right now, she is on her way!

I took the deepest breath and pushed one last time. And after a few seconds, the room was silent except for my baby's cries.

"You have yourself a baby girl."

All of my fears and insecurities had to leave the room that day. Her wide eyes pierced the depths of my soul. Her round cheeks were covered in months of the sorrow I allowed into my life, but she was here for a purpose. Maddison introduced me to womanhood.

I spent the first night in the hospital with only my baby girl. I wanted her dad there, but she was all I *needed*. She gave me a reason to exist.

The nurse asked if I wanted her to be taken to the nursery so I could rest.

I declined her offer. I needed my daughter that night.

After the birth of Maddison I moved in with my sister and her boyfriend. A couple weeks after her birth my bonus mom came down to bring some things and check on us. She held Maddison and said, "I'm in love." My life wasn't going the way I envisioned it, but I was undoubtedly surrounded by love. I only lived with Nerra and her boyfriend for a short period of time before I started to look for an apartment. My expectations for Wade were low because there were still feelings attached and I didn't want to be disappointed. When he called to ask if he could keep her over the weekend I let him. When he called to check on her I gave him updates. I attempted to keep things cordial although I still truly loved him. I hated seeing him with his other family because he didn't even look my way. At this point, we were strictly business.

I told my parents that I found an apartment, but I needed help furnishing it. I didn't have to say much because decorating and interior design were my bonus mom's thing. She pulled some things together and we set a date for when they would drive down and help us get settled in. A few weeks later, they had fully furnished my first apartment. Anything that was needed, they did for us.

There was one window in the living room that my bonus mom hung the thickest curtains against. You could tell by how heavy the fabric was that these curtains were of good quality. They were burnt orange, blocked out every ounce of light, and hung low to the ground. I had two cream-colored couches with accent tables and pillows. My apartment was cozy. Maddison's room didn't have a baby bed because she slept with me. I hung all of her tiny clothes up in the closet in her room. Against the wall there was a small changing table, a few boxes of diapers, and baby toys we had received from my baby shower.

It was just me and my daughter against the world. For months I ate, breathed, and slept Maddison. I realized that I had begun to neglect myself because I thought that was the right thing to do. Many women who become mothers feel as though their life is over once they have a child. I'm here to tell you that it is okay to eat, breathe, and sleep your children, but adult interaction and time to yourself is a MUST. I was afraid to let Maddison out of my sight. I went by the book from how to do feedings down to the number of diapers she was supposed to soil a day. I do believe that having children should change your outlook on life as a woman, especially raising daughters. There are certain things that are acceptable and certain things that you have to step away from. I just felt like, at the time, I shouldn't be taking any time for myself because that time is time that I could be pouring into my daughter. I should be bonding, reading to her, and just being a mother 24 hours a day, 7 days a week, right? What I didn't realize is that this was not healthy behavior. How could I give her 100% when I was drained most of the time and not taking time out for myself, just to breathe? I believe that moms should take time for themselves, even if it is just to go get a pedicure or go have lunch with a girlfriend. Take care of you.

Wade was permanently living with Linda, but we started to flirt when he came to pick Maddison up. This was dangerous because

I was allowing him to run my house while he lived with another woman. He didn't spend much time at my new apartment at first, but he made sure to come get his daughter every weekend. During the week when he worked he came by on his lunch. He was winning as a father, but failing as the best friend and first real love that I thought I knew.

After the doctor cleared me during my 6 weeks checkup, I knew I was about to hit the streets. There was a party every weekend. I told Wade that I needed him to keep the baby because I was going out one weekend. If you have experienced country life then you know what it means to pull up to the hood store before you go out to any function. You might catch your boo, baby daddy, or that girl that don't like you up there and you had to show all of 'em who you are. As soon as I stepped out the car I heard, "Damn, Black." Wade was standing in front of the store.

"Um, sir, why are you out and where is my baby?" I was annoyed.

"Man, she at home with Linda, she's straight," he said with a sneaky smirk.

"You do too much," I said and walked off. I wasn't worried about him, I was ready to party.

It was homecoming weekend and for Hillsboro that meant new hair styles, new outfits, and it was a must to be outside the whole weekend. Saturday night was the only night that mattered. That's when you put on your "get your head knocked off" dress. The one that made your man or the baby daddy you were still sexing jealous enough to knock your head off. And I had mine ready.

I felt somebody come up behind me in the party and grab my waist.

"Stop playing with me in here."

I turned around to see Wade looking good enough to eat and smelling even better.

"Boy, go home to your woman," I said while moving his hands from around me.

"I'm going home with you tonight. Tell them other ones to move around," he said.

My crazy ass did just that. I had a lil dude I was dealing with, but it was nothing serious. He caught me at the wrong time in life. I was hurting so all I knew how to do was hurt people.

After the party I shot straight home. I was thinking to myself how the hell is he going to come over here when Maddison is at home with his woman? I knew he was spending the night because why wouldn't he? I wasn't just a slide through, I was Porcia.

Well, he slid his ass right through and left. He didn't even turn his car off.

We didn't use a condom this time, and I felt it.

Now that we were back fooling around often I became the baby mama from hell. I was the baby mama that called his phone back-to-back if he didn't answer, even if I knew he was home with his woman. After about 35 (no exaggeration) ignored phone calls I would send long text messages. I would write out the texts and just hit send on the same message over and over until it froze his phone up (we had sidekicks and razors back then). After all of that, he would finally call back and I would say something stupid like, "Maddison's pink shirt is missing. Y'all need to return all my baby stuff." Just the most unnecessary stuff. I was just making up random stuff to get him to give me some kind of reaction. I would show up to their house and be hella disrespectful. I wouldn't speak to his girl and I would start arguments with him. It got so bad that we had to start meeting at his mama's house and go through her to exchange the baby. Because I was hurt, I wanted to disrupt his whole world. I even went through a phase where I kept him from seeing Maddison for dumb reasons. My hurt turned into anger and I turned outrageous. He would call to get her and I would just simply say no. "No, because you did this to **ME** and you hurt **ME**. You over there with that other girl and you hurt **MY** feelings." He had never done anything to harm my baby and he was ready to be a father, but I was too hung up on my feelings.

A couple of months went by and I missed my period. I took a pregnancy test and I was pregnant. Maddison was all of 4 months old and here I was pregnant again. A part of me was afraid, but the other part of me thought that because I was having another one of his kids that I had somehow trapped him. It seemed like the second he found out I was pregnant again he just did a complete turnaround. He called me every name under the sun, told me that the baby wasn't his, and if it was I should get rid of it because it was already dead to him. He told me that he would have nothing to do with the kid at all. I battled with myself about whether I should keep the baby, because an abortion was just out of the question. The last straw was when he stopped taking my calls. He wouldn't even speak to me about Maddison anymore and I was just left all alone. I picked up the phone and made the hardest decision. I scheduled an appointment to have an abortion. Wade's sister was the only person there and she held my hand while I aborted what would have been our second child. This is one of the things that I wish I could go back and redo. I had dreams about babies every night for months after having the procedure. After doing it, I felt a piece of me had died. The love I once had for Wade was sucked right out of me right along with the baby. I still loved him, but I looked at him differently from that day on.

Maddison was about 6 months old when I received a call from J. One weekend he told me he was going to Austin for something and Hillsboro was on the way so he wanted to stop by. It felt weird because we had not been in the same space with one another in a really long time. When he got there, I could quickly tell that he had grown a lot. He was so gentle and patient. When Maddison was fussy he walked around the room and rocked her to sleep. It was beautiful. We didn't take anything past that night. We just lived in that moment and the next morning he was on his way.

Despite the many challenges in me and Wade's relationship, Maddison was my top priority. The relationship between a father and his daughter is her first example of how she should be treated by a man. I knew I had to get it together soon for her. If you are reading this and you are keeping your child away from their father because of something he did to *you*, just stop it. Trust me, I know it's easier said than done because when we are hurt we want them to suffer, but it should not be at the expense of your child. Fix it, so you won't be doing damage control on a messed-up teenager because *you* were mad. Had I kept up the shenanigans, my daughter would be missing out on all the fun times and all the father daughter moments with him. Why let all of that time go by and let the child miss out on a bond and a relationship with their father? All because you're mad. Let it go, sis. AND take those much-needed breaks. Once I came to my senses and got out my feelings, things went so smoothly. Wade got Maddison every other weekend, came to chill with her during the week, and we rotated holidays.

Chapter 5

MY MARIE

WADE stepped things up in the fatherhood area, but I still wanted him as my man. I was running out of reasons to get him to talk to me. Nothing seemed to affect him. The only time he showed his disdain towards anything was if there was another man involved. I had to make him see me.

Nerra's boyfriend was friends with everybody. Every time I stopped by to visit, there was someone there playing the game with him. One night I went to visit and there was this guy sitting on the couch. Maddison was with Wade for the night. The only plan I had was to go back to my apartment and watch reruns of *Friends*. What I needed to be doing was getting to the root of why I couldn't just enjoy my own company. The need to bounce from situation to situation wasn't the best feeling.

Looks are one thing, but you can tell a lot when someone opens their mouth to speak. I started to observe this guy. He didn't speak much. There was this mystery about him that intrigued me. The kind that your mother tells you to stay away from. I wasn't looking for a serious relationship, I was too damaged. I needed companionship and

I wanted revenge. I needed something to do but I wanted him. Wade would for sure feel this one. Me and the new guy exchanged numbers. We talked through text messages and a couple of phone calls. The first night I invited him over we talked about all kinds of stuff, including who he knew in town. It turned out that his siblings and my cousin Tonya's best friends shared the same father. I knew his family well. I didn't remember him being around when we were younger, but I knew his whole family. He went on to tell me how he did not meet his brother and sisters until they were adults. The town he was from was only a couple of hours up the road. His mother's family was from Tyler, Texas. The more we talked the more I started to realize that I actually had seen him before. It didn't dawn on me at first, but the first time I saw him was at a party. My instincts told me that getting with him wasn't the best idea, but my need for revenge and company made me develop a fast relationship with him.

Anything I wanted he would buy it for me. Anytime I needed help with Maddison he handed over stacks of money for her. He told me about his kids and his baby mamas in Tyler. He had a lot of baggage, but I wasn't trying to marry him. He was fun. We kicked it hard. I wasn't a smoker but I did whatever with him. One night we were high and I noticed him staring at me. "Girl, I am fertile," he said laughing. "If I get some on your foot it's bound to run up your leg and you'll be pregnant." Despite him saying this I did *not* proceed with caution.

A couple of drunk nights and a few missed periods later, I knew I had to take a test. I was pregnant with my second child by another man.

He left when I was about 3 months pregnant, but I didn't shed one tear over him. I had no true feelings for him. He served his purpose and I got caught up. I fell right into the hole I thought I was digging for Wade. My pride was my worst enemy and it got me every single time. Here I was with a child still in diapers and one on the way. No job, rent was due, electricity was cut off every week, and I couldn't handle it anymore. I had to pull myself out of this cycle. The tips I made at my waitressing job were barely enough to feed us, let alone pay bills. I needed money and I needed it fast.

I made my way to the first strip club and "applied" for a position. I was very tiny with my second daughter. My stomach was completely flat the first few months. I didn't start showing until I was about 6 months or so. It wasn't really an application at the strip club; you just walked into this hell hole and were told to spin around as if you were a car on a showroom floor. When the owner gives you the okay, you get on the stage and "audition" for the job. The first time I had to dance and have strangers touch me and talk to me in a sexual way was the most degrading feeling. I felt so low, but the money I was making was enough to buy diapers and I didn't have to depend on anyone for anything. I won't lie, at one point I was enjoying making the money because not only could I buy Maddison what she needed, but I could also get her things that she wanted.

I knew I had no business doing the things that I was doing, but my pride wouldn't let me ask for help. This is the part of living life on your own terms that isn't so pretty. You can't make decisions at the expense of others. I didn't want to walk around feeling entitled to anything just because I was related to someone. If not wanting to lean on others to help fix my mistakes is not obvious enough, I can take it a step further. I don't like asking for help in fear of it being brought up again. It's like this, you already feel low when you have to ask for help, then to turn around and be reminded that you were helped is the lowest feeling. So with my pride in tow, I went into survival mode. I would go to the store and just take whatever I couldn't afford to buy. I thank God on a daily basis that I didn't get caught up in my mess. I could have landed myself in jail.

The only time I cried when I was pregnant with Kennedy was when I was about 7 months and that was only because I let myself get into the same situation. Not only did I allow myself to get pregnant by someone I didn't love, I was now about to be a mother of two. I heard from Kennedy's father around that same month, excuse me, I heard from his WIFE, with whom he had three other children. She contacted me to let me know that he would no longer be returning to me and my "BASTARD" child. The childish games started from there.

She would "accidentally" call me while they were having sex, call me while he was bad mouthing me so that I could hear the things that he was saying, the list goes on. This is one of the times in my life where I was very cold hearted, so those things didn't bother me. I would just hang up the phone and eventually I blocked both of their numbers. The things that I had been through had caused me to put up a wall. I didn't feel anything. I didn't care about anything or anybody and I wasn't afraid to speak my mind. The passive, sweet, innocent girl was slowly dying and I wasn't trying to save her.

Kennedy Marie's birth was way different than Maddison's. October 16, 2009 was the day. I only stayed in labor with her for about 45 minutes and I felt every bit of pain. By the time I got the epidural it was already too late; she was on her way into this already complicated world. My mother and Nerra were in the delivery room this time and I felt safe. Mama prayed for my delivery to go smoothly while Nerra tried to calm me down with jokes. You know how women embrace the birth of their babies and how they are so overjoyed when it's time to go home and start this new journey called motherhood? Yeah, I didn't get that feeling at all. Kennedy was special and I knew it the moment I looked at her, but I wasn't ready to leave the hospital, where, at the push of a button, I could have someone come in and take the baby to the nursery so I could get an hour of rest.

My Marie was the smallest bundle of love. Her hair was jet black and silky. I instantly fell in love with her. What I didn't know is that my smallest child would have the biggest personality. The little girl in me feels liberated when I look at Marie today. At the age of 11 she's so unapologetically herself. A natural leader who will disown you if you play with her family.

The day I got out of the hospital didn't feel real. There was no one available to drive me home so I packed myself, Maddison, and Kennedy into my 2-door cougar and we headed to my parents' house. Sonya, my bonus mom's niece, and her children were living there at the time and she offered to help me with Maddison and the new baby. I didn't want any sympathy from anybody because my girls were my responsibility, but I was in no place to turn down the help. I knew staying with her and letting her help me was the best decision because babies are just drawn to Sonya for some reason. She has that touch. I would be holding Kennedy trying to soothe her and the cries wouldn't stop. Sonya would come in to get her and she would instantly stop crying. I didn't even feel bad for myself, I was just happy that my baby was comfortable. My energy was off and Kennedy sensed that. Sonya really helped me out more than she knows. She comforted me when I started to feel down.

A couple of days into my stay, Kennedy became even more fussy. It seemed like every time I touched her she cringed like she was in pain. She would whimper and cry on and off until I put her down to sleep. Her pain progressed over time and she was full out crying. I couldn't burp her after a feeding because that required me to pat and rub her back. She was in so much pain. I decided to go to the local children's hospital because I was afraid. Someone that new and tiny couldn't possibly handle such pain. I packed a diaper bag for Kennedy, grabbed my phone charger, and we were on our way. Maddison would stay at my parents' house with Sonya. She was safe there so I didn't worry about that. All of my focus shifted to Kennedy. Once we arrived at the hospital the nurses went through all of their protocols and then put us into a room. The doctor came in shortly after I got settled in. Kennedy was diagnosed with Respiratory Syncytial Virus. The doctor asked if I had anyone who could bring me extra clothes for the baby and I because we weren't going home that night. It wasn't a deadly diagnosis, but she was a newborn so they wanted to monitor her.

Cooks Children's Hospital was a very hospitable place. We were assigned a room. The room had a tiny bed for Kennedy and I slept in the big bed. I wasn't supposed to put her in the bed with me, but I needed to bond with her. A representative from the hospital came in to go over how the next few days would go. I was given meal tickets, a small pillow that had been handmade by a local charity, and more comfort than I received at the hospital Kennedy was born in. I felt like everything was going to be okay. I didn't watch much television because I didn't have cable. *Friends* and *Sex in the City* came on the free channel so those were my shows. When Kennedy was awake I prayed over her and talked to her. When I fed her I made sure to speak life into her. She was special.

After about a week we ended our stay there. I stayed a few extra days at my parents' house before I made my way back to Hillsboro. I needed to get back home to unpack. I no longer had my own apartment so I would be going home to the apartment with my mother and grandmother, and Nerra would stop in every once in a while.

I didn't work for the first three months of being a mother to a toddler and a newborn. I received federal aid and I had an application on file to receive public housing when my name came up on the list. My mother prayed over my children and I daily. Her prayers were not the cute two-minute prayers either. She'd lay face down on the floor asking God to cover her family. She and my grandmother took good care of us. My grandmother would prepare Thanksgiving style meals on random days. She didn't have to cook, but she loved feeding her family.

We had reached another new year and I knew that it was time for me to get a job and find an apartment for my girls and I. I was never pressured to move out by my mother. She always found the best way to put things on my radar and I appreciate her for that. Although I loved her for her empathy and patience, I didn't want to take advantage of her heart.

My mother came home one day and asked me if I had ever given any thought into getting a certified nursing assistant license. I hadn't. I had no idea what a CNA's job consisted of. I began to do a little research and I talked to my friend Denekia about it. She was going through rough seasons in her life as well so we both were on a quest to do better financially. I signed up to take the classes at a nursing home that was about fifteen minutes away from my mom's apartment. We went through the application process and soon after, we were given specific job details and a schedule. I immediately thought about the girls; I needed to report to class at six o'clock in the morning where

I would remain until 3 p.m. so I was going to need a babysitter and I was going to have to ask my mother and grandmother. Wade would get Maddison every weekend and if I asked him during the week he never said no. Kennedy on the other hand only had me.

There was no hesitation from them. They instantly agreed to look after my daughters for almost 10 hours a day Monday through Friday for the next eight weeks. There are certain time periods that are a blur to me. My life moved so fast at times that I didn't really stop and let things soak in. Denekia and I had a routine. We had a goal to accomplish. Our days started at 5 a.m. so we didn't hang out on the weekends. Our "hanging out" was occasionally going to Bingo after class.

We flew through the program and eight weeks later, it was time to take the state test. The week of the state test Maddison had a bad asthma flare up so I had to call out of work. We weren't allowed to miss, but this was out of my control. I needed to be home with my sick child. I was subsequently fired for this. All of the hard work and early mornings I put in were on their way down the drain. Fortunately however, my mother's words and prayers make things happen. I was 22 years old at the time, but I still needed my mom because I had pretty much given up. She got on the phone with the staff at the nursing home and let them have it. She explained to them that I was a single mother trying to make a living to support myself and my children. Mama didn't have any conversation with anyone without bringing God up. She began to minister to one of the nurses and it softened her up some. The conversation went from intense to compassionate. I wasn't privy to the entire conversation, but I was able to take my state test that week.

On the test there was a written portion as well as a physical portion. For those eight weeks we had spent time learning how to properly shave a male resident's beard, the correct way to make the residents' beds, as well as help them shower and get dressed. I paid the most attention when the instructor started to go over how to change a bed pad or diaper. Learning how to move a resident from the bed to a wheelchair took precision. You could really mess up your back if you didn't follow the correct procedure, and dropping someone was out of the question. Doing this job meant taking on a huge responsibility. There were people who put their trust into the nurses and staff at these facilities. This was a job I had to take seriously. These were the lives of elderly people who had been teachers and doctors, but most importantly they couldn't fend for themselves. I treated them like they were my grandparents. I didn't have much patience with people, but I didn't play that when it came to elderly people. I was on their time.

I passed my state test and soon after I was cleared to work as a CNA at the nursing home I trained at. My time there humbled me in so many ways. I met some amazing nurses and some not so nice CNA's. There are people who will purposely neglect your loved ones out of pure laziness, but I treated every resident with love and respect, even when they became anxious. Bath time for some people is normally the time to unwind and relax, but if you are bed ridden it takes a lot out of you. The elderly residents hated bath time. The winter time was the worst. I had a lady punch me because I came into her room and told her it was her shower time.

"It's too damn cold to get in that water," she said.

She hadn't had a shower in two days, and although I was thrown off by her punch, I had to make it happen. I let her talk it out as I went about her room finding her a fresh pair of clothes to slip into after her shower. I gathered her lotion and creams and a comfortable pair of socks. I never stopped talking to her while I gathered her things. She eventually gave up and agreed to let me assist her in taking a shower. In those moments my character was built. Only compassion and understanding will help you get through some of the roughest days of this type of work.

My schedule changed after I had officially become a CNA. I worked four days on and two days off from 6 a.m. - 2 p.m. My grandmother and mother had also settled into a routine with the girls. By the time I made it home from work my daughters were bathed, dressed, and their hair was slicked down. My mother would be doing with them, the same thing she did with Nerra and I when we were little. After your appearance was together it was time for positive affirmations, scripture, and a daily prayer. I thought because my mother was younger that she would take on the responsibility of the newborn but my granny had it together. Kennedy had become her favorite. She would wash Kennedy's onesies in the sink and hang them out to dry. She found joy in matching her onesie with a fancy headband and laying her down for a nap. By the time Kennedy was six months old my granny talked to her like she understood what was going on. After work I took the weight off of them, but my mother would still come into the room to help me straighten up or watch the baby while I showered. Every night my grandmother came into the room to tell us goodnight, but she spent extra time holding Kennedy and staring into her eyes before she would kiss her goodnight.

My life wasn't perfect on paper, but I was surrounded by love and the best damn support system anyone could ask for. I would work during the day, be in full mommy mode in the afternoon, and some nights I went to Bingo.

The girls were growing. Maddison was coming into her own silly personality and Kennedy was fully crawling and pulling up on things at nine months old. She bypassed baby food and went straight to beans, mashed potatoes, and whatever else my granny was eating. They were two peas in a pod.

Although I was grateful, my living situation had to change. I could not be a mother of two children living with my mother and grandmother. Our circumstances were not ideal but they bonded us. My mother's prayers along with my grandmother's wisdom (and food) made my time there relaxed, but I knew that it was time for me to find an apartment for my girls and I.

It didn't take me long to find a place for me and my girls. I found a tiny two-story apartment on the other side of town. When it was finally time for us to move across town into our new apartment Kennedy cried. She had begun to cry every time we left my granny. They were attached. You could see the joy in her eyes when my granny entered a room. That was real love.

My sister Tia had driven down to help us get moved. I lost most of the furniture my parents gave me for my first apartment due to an unpaid storage bill. My high school diploma along with all of my athletic accomplishments and medals were gone. The furniture I had was still in good shape, but most of the quality pieces I had in my first apartment were no more.

The door of our new apartment was red. When you walked into the apartment you stepped right into the living room. To the left were two sets of stairs that led to the two bedrooms upstairs. Just past the living room was the kitchen and the back door. Our first night there was very strange. Not strange in the way that things happened, but it was an unfamiliar place.

I got everything unpacked on the first day but it took me a few months to get used to living in our new apartment.

JOURNAL ENTRY

I received a call from Kennedy's dad when she was 3 months old. He asked if he could come see his new daughter for the first time. The time to be present would have been when she was born, but I wasn't a selfish person. I agreed to let him come visit her. She was just a baby so we sat in silence for a minute before I started to let him have it. The conversation consisted of me describing her birth, him apologizing for not being there, and a bunch of other empty promises. I knew that much.

Regardless of my relationship or lack thereof with him, I won't ever bad mouth him to Kennedy. That will end up doing more damage in the long run. Always think of the big picture when it comes to absent fathers. A daughter without a father can grow up two different ways. She will either spend her time searching for that love from a man or she will stand ten toes down and make better decisions. Kennedy is a natural born leader and God chose her. As she gets older I might allow him to be in her life if he's consistent. If she decides to pursue a relationship with her father when she is an adult I will be standing right beside her encouraging it. Unity and healing in Black families will always be something I support.

January 2010

JOURNAL ENTRY

How come nobody told me that losing someone to prison feels like a death in the family? The bond that Wade and I have is one that can never be broken nor duplicated. We grew up together. My daddy was right about Wade, but he will never understand the connection I felt with the father of my first-born daughter. My experience with love as a youngin was like the ones you read in those Sistah Souljah novels. That shit was classic and I don't regret any of it. How can I? I have Maddison.

The relationship between a father and his daughter is her first example of how she should be treated by a man. He wasn't just a weekend dad, he built a healthy relationship with my daughter and her brother and sisters. Arrissa, Arrya, and Bubba are bound to my daughter by blood for life and that connection for Maddison means everything.

IN 2017 WADE WAS SENTENCED TO 25 YEARS IN PRISON.

My first reaction to getting the news that he would spend the next 25 years behind bars was SHOCK. I couldn't believe it. I've always known karma would get him, but I never imagined his karma getting us all.

This experience stained the depths of my soul and I'll probably be spending my entire life trying to mend those wounds. Since his sentencing my emotions have been all over the place. I'm so mad at him. So fucking hurt. How could he be so careless? Before he was sent away I took Maddison to see him. He needed to be the one to tell her that their time together was about to be put on hold until she's an adult. Her teen years are not supposed to be spent crying herself to sleep for months.

Children can be so forgiving and they have the purest hearts. "Mama, he made a mistake and should be forgiven for that," is what she told me. She prays for God to work out a miracle for her dad and I encourage her to do so. I have to. When I tell her the stories of our young love she laughs from a healthy place. I try my hardest to keep her spirits up. Some days my emotions get in the way and I get sad. She doesn't see the tears I shed but she feels them. She can't read my thoughts, but when I'm having one of those days she will randomly come talk about things her dad has taught her. The connection is WILD!!

One day she came into my room and said, "Mama, I know my daddy is your friend too and I just want to make sure you're okay too." THAT MELTED MY HEART!

She's so much stronger than I imagined she would be. One day she will know that her strength introduced me to a stronger me.

Wade, our story is a classic. Our daughter is the proof...

—P
Nov. 4, 2018

Chapter 6

AND THEN THERE WERE 3

K ENNEDY was coming up on 8 months and I was finally able to exhale. I had settled into a routine. My circumstances were not ideal, but I was making it work. I still worked as a CNA and since I lived across town now I had to start my mornings earlier. I would get up at 4 a.m. to get the girls ready to go to my mother and grandmother's apartment. The night before I made sure to pack extra clothes, snacks, and food for them. When I wasn't caring for elderly residents I was caring for a baby and a toddler. My days went this same way Monday through Friday. Single parents wear many hats and I think that it is important for us, whether you are a single mom or dad, to take time for ourselves. I'm not saying it is ok to go out and party every weekend and forget that you are a parent, but having a glass of wine every now and then or going to a spa does not spell neglect.

One morning while I was driving to work I told Denekia that I needed to get out. *We* needed to get out. Denekia was married and her husband played no games so she would just be going for the sake of getting out the house.

Like most small towns, there was an even bigger country town a few miles away where you went if you wanted to experience "night life." Waco, Texas was it for us. I hadn't been clubbing in Waco in a very long time because almost every time we went out there was a fight or someone started shooting, and my old nerves couldn't take a lot of that anymore.

I didn't even see Rhileey's father coming. I had tunnel vision in the motherhood area of my life, but for some reason I felt like I needed more action. My third daughter's father is four years younger than me so when we met he was REALLY young. Now before you judge me, let me explain. Leroy was young, but his spirit is what attracted me to him. Ok, it may have also been the fact that he was an amazing dancer and effortlessly funny.

The club wasn't the place I wanted to find a companion but that's where it happened. Leroy was with a group of guys and they all danced around the whole night. Denekia and I kind of laughed because the men we were used to dealing with were too cool to dance. "Hurry up and put my number in your phone," he said. I was only in my early 20s, but I was too old to be playing these games. Still, I played along and put my number in his phone. It didn't take long for us to connect and eventually start going out on dates. Our first date was a disaster and I ignored so many red flags. We planned to go see a movie, but since he didn't have a car we planned for me to meet him in Waco. At the time I didn't care about driving to him because I just wanted to be out on a date that bad. The day came and we talked for most of the day. I made sure to call him to double check to see if we were still good for the movie date and he assured me that we were. There was a weird feeling that came over me, but I attributed it to the fact that this was my first date with a new guy. I was halfway to Waco and I decided to call him one last time to get his location. It would take me about 15 minutes to get to the theatre so I wanted to make sure our arrivals were close. The phone rang and rang and rang. The third call was when things started to register. I was being stood up. I had *never* been stood up before, so honestly it was comical to me. All I could think about was when I made it back to Hillsboro how bad Nerra was about to laugh because that was the type of stuff we laughed about.

Because I had already purchased my movie ticket, I decided to go see the movie alone. There was no need to waste that money on top of the gas I already burned up to drive the 30 minutes to Waco. After I got my popcorn I found my way to my seat in the theater. There was a family sitting directly behind me and I heard one of the younger girls call out a familiar name. When Leroy and I would be on the phone he talked about his mom and sisters a lot. So much so that I knew their names. We weren't at the "meet the family" level so I had never laid eyes on his family so I didn't know what they looked like. I thought it was just a coincidence and I said to myself there had to be more than one Amber and Ebony in Waco, Texas. The more they talked the clearer things became. The new guy stood me up, and I was sitting in front of his mother and sisters at the movie theater. I didn't dare turn around and introduce myself. What was I going to say? "Hello. Your son and brother stood me up on our date tonight, but it's so nice to finally meet you." I spared myself the humiliation and sat through the movie by myself. I already knew that I would not be calling him back.

The next day my phone rang and one of his friends was on the other end. "Leroy went to jail last night," he said. I listened attentively on the other end while rolling my eyes. These young niggas had no clue how to do this. Lying about going to jail was the oldest trick in the book and I had already heard he was in Austin that night for The Texas Relays. I turned down my sister's invitation to go to the Texas Relays so that I could go to the movies with him and he went anyway? What was my life becoming? My need for a companion and some good penis was making me look really dumb. I know what you are thinking, "She blocked his number and went on with her life, right?" Wrong. I wasn't that smart, yet. He finally called and joked and charmed his way back into my head. After all, it was just one bad first date.

Although Leroy was young, he knew how to do the family thing. I never hid the fact that I had two daughters and he didn't seem to mind. When I would go to Waco he would ask if I was bringing the kids. I watched how he interacted with the girls to see if there were any weird vibes, but I never got any. He spent his off days in Hillsboro with us and it felt like a little family. Maddison was with Wade every other weekend so the majority of the time it was just us and Kennedy. For him to have been so young and not have any children, he was very patient. There were things that I would yell about that he would simply say with a calm tone that helped Kennedy get it together. Who sent this man?

It was rare that I had a full kid free weekend so when I did I took full advantage of the empty house. Leroy was coming to stay and I planned on sexing him up and down that apartment all weekend. I didn't want any more children, but the unhealed part of me wanted to give him a child. I had enough experience in this area to know that having a child by a man does not keep him around so that wasn't my reason. I also knew that I was having a hard time raising the two I already had and adding a third child to my life wasn't the best idea. Even though I was aware of all of these things, the good sex had me feeling some kind of way and soon enough Rhileey was conceived. I was about to be a mother of 3 children and it didn't even matter to me because, again, I thought I was in love.

My pregnancy with my third child was different. I already had two girls so it was natural that I prayed for this one to be a boy. Leroy had mixed feelings because this was going to be his first child. He didn't care what the gender was, he was more concerned about bringing a baby into this twisted world. I was afraid that his reservations about it all would cause him to run like Kennedy's dad did, but he stayed. He was present for doctors' visits, made late night food runs, and often rubbed my belly and talked to our growing child.

My mother and grandmother suspected that I was pregnant weeks before they sat me down. One day I was picking the girls up from their apartment and my granny stopped me at the door. "Your stomach is looking mighty round, Porcia D," she said. I knew then that she already knew. I started to cry and she stopped me and put her hands on my shoulders. "You have to start making better choices, baby, but don't cry. God will take care of you with this one just like He did these last two," she said. I wiped my tears and hugged her. "You need to go in there and tell Deshon," she said. My mother wasn't judgmental so I knew her response to me being pregnant with my third child would be light. I was semi-right. The moment I told her I saw worry fall over her. She fell silent and I knew I was about to be flooded with a lecture. Once she gathered her thoughts she said to me that I needed to consider getting my tubes tied after this baby. I wasn't married and I didn't even know if Leroy was the person I was going to marry, but I couldn't agree with her more. Three children was enough. She held me as I cried, and then she said those dreadful words, "You know you need to call your dad and tell him, right?" I knew I needed to, but I didn't feel like I was my parents' favorite person at the time because of the choices I was making in my life so I wasn't exactly excited about sharing the news.

I didn't rely on them for financial support, I handled my own responsibilities. I never called them to ask them to look after my children so I could go run the streets or any of that. My life wasn't the best, but I was taking care of my children because I knew they were my responsibility. Eventually I mustered up the strength to make the call to tell my parents that I was about to be a mother of three. I called my bonus mom's phone to tell her first and the response she gave me cut me deeply. "You are not going to be able to take care of three children, Porcia, I suggest you get an abortion," she said. I instantly became defensive because how could she say that to me? I was confused because she always made the comment that she was the last to know about all of my pregnancies. This is why. I knew the response I would get would damage me more than it helped me. I disregarded what she said and decided that I would take care of my kids like I had been doing. I was going to prove her wrong.

That was the phone call that made me isolate myself even more. I didn't expect her response to be the happiest one because the responses I got about my previous pregnancies were not the most pleasant, but I never expected her to suggest an abortion. When my brother had his first son I remember my parents posting to their social media saying, "The king is here." They looked so happy to be having another grandchild and I couldn't help but feel envious. When his daughter was about to be born my bonus mom threw my sister-in-law the most beautiful baby shower I had ever seen. There was so much love in the room for their baby girl and all I wanted was to feel that with my bonus mom. I already aborted one child after Maddison was born and that haunted me for months, so there was no way that it would happen ever again. The baby that was growing inside of me was just as special as the first two I gave birth to.

Leroy's mom came down to my apartment so that we could meet in person when I was about 8 months pregnant. We talked over the phone a few times but I was having her grandchild so it was important to both of us that we met in person. I didn't know what type of grandmother she would be so I was skeptical about starting this journey with her. When she came she brought Leroy's sister, Amber, who was also pregnant. She would have two grandchildren born in the same month, possibly days apart. The only thing I knew about his mother was that she was a Jehovah's witness. I also knew that they did not celebrate holidays and my apartment was a winter wonderland. I had the biggest festive tree and she was on her way to my house. I wasn't trying to hide anything, I just wanted to make sure she was comfortable. My anxiety had me unplugging the Christmas lights like that would make a difference. I wanted to make a good impression, but I also wanted to let her know what type of mother I was. I wasn't one of the ones who had the babies and counted on the grandparents to raise them. I had a support system, but my daughters were my responsibility.

We sat in my living room and talked for hours. Amber didn't say too much but her spirit was calm. I didn't take her silence personally because we were strangers, but I enjoyed talking to Leroy's mom. She assured me that she would drive down for Rhileey's birth.

Towards the end of my pregnancy my parents came around. They wanted to spend time with Maddison and Kennedy and there was no way I would come in between that. Their disdain for my life choices did not affect the way they showed up as grandparents. They came down to visit and drop off gifts for the girls from time to time. Occasionally we shared a laugh, but my heart was hardened so I didn't take the opportunity to open up to them. There was always this nervous energy when they would come around and I constantly felt the need to put on a facade. I needed to appear that I had my life in order because I knew that they thought the opposite. Christmas was approaching and I had no intention of going down to see them. My due date was in December so I didn't have to come up with a bogus reason about why I didn't want to be around for the holidays.

When I found out that the new baby would be another girl, I cried. I wanted a son so badly. What was I going to do with 3 daughters? Leroy was just happy to have a healthy baby on the way. The day of my last appointment is the day I was supposed to give birth, but Rhileey had other plans. She was still very high in my womb and I hadn't dilated past 2 centimeters. Frustration set in because I was beyond ready to have my body to myself again. I begged my doctor to do something to speed up the process and he suggested that I take the entire weekend to relax. "Relax yourself because life with a new baby is about to be rough." I told him that I would take his advice, but I had other plans. There was a hill at the city park that would bring a grown man to his knees and in my case, bring on some strong labor pains. I walked that hill twice a day trying to kick start my labor, but it didn't help at all. I decided to beg my doctor some more. Since I had hit 40 weeks he scheduled an induction for the following Monday.

Sunday night I double checked my hospital bag and we waited. I didn't get any sleep that night. Although I had done this before, I was just as nervous as the first time. There was no large crowd waiting for Rhileey to be born, It was only me and Leroy. My parents weren't able to come down, my family that was in town had to work, and his mother made it to the hospital too late. She was livid because she had never missed the birth of a grandchild.

Leroy held my hand and kissed my forehead when it was time to push. This was a new child but the feeling was the same. The signals that my body gave off when it was time to push were very familiar. After coming to grips with the fact that the only thing that was about to move through you was an almost 8-pound baby you begin to feel light headed and nauseous. I wasn't ready but she was on her way. It only took a few pushes and then I heard my baby cry. Her cries relieved me. I had given birth to my last daughter and she was healthy. The sparkle I saw in Leroy's eyes while he held his daughter for the first time melted me. I wondered what type of father he would be. Would he leave after the newness of this whole thing wore off? I almost let my thoughts run wild, but I caught myself and chose to stay in the moment.

We stayed up all night staring at our daughter. I needed to get some rest but my heart was full. To the left of me in her crib was my baby girl and to the right of me Leroy was stretched out on the tiny hospital couch. I had decided to put Rhileey in her crib once I got her to sleep so Leroy could come in the bed with me. Those are the moments I'll cherish forever. No matter what happened and what was coming, I'll always remember feeling connected that night.

Around 6:00 a.m. the nurses came in to take Rhileey to the nursery while I was taken back for the procedure. I was aware that I would be putting a stop to the baby factory for good. I didn't regret my decision until I was given the anesthesia. What if I wanted to have more children? What if Leroy and I didn't work out? The questions I had no longer mattered because the medicine began to kick in and I was on my way out. I don't know if the medicine was that strong or if I was just tired from being up all-night staring at Rhileey and Leroy, but I was out cold.

The next day the doctor came in to check my scar out. They had to cut a small incision underneath my belly button so he wanted to inspect the site. I prayed that all was well because I was ready to go home. Leroy left after I came out of surgery and I gave him the look of death. He felt it and promised me he was coming right back to drive us home from the hospital. I thought I was in a better place, but the past traumas I experienced made me not believe him. My hormones were all over the place and I cried as soon as he walked out the door.

While I waited, the nurses slipped Rhileey into a Christmas stocking for her first photos and it was perfect. The moment I saw the photo I couldn't wait to make an ornament out of it that read "Rhileey's first Christmas." My life felt complete.

Once I signed the discharge papers Leroy came walking through the door and I felt relieved. He kept his word and we were on our way home with our new baby. My mother and grandmother were looking after Maddison and Kennedy during the whole process. I didn't have to worry because I knew my mom had them reading scriptures and quoting positive affirmations the same way she did when I was just a girl. My grandmother loved to cook Sunday style meals every day of the week so food wasn't something I had to worry about either.

When we all got settled in at home I was no longer a "by the book" mom. I got rid of that very quickly. When you have a newborn you are on their time. When I needed to take a shower or wash dishes, I would let Maddison feed Rhileey. Things I would have frowned upon before, I didn't give a lot of energy or thought to because it was starting to stress me out. Instead of going behind the girls picking up every toy they pulled out, I would let them play with every toy in the toy box, jump, scream, and make as much noise as they wanted and then when it was their bedtime, I would bathe them, lay them in bed, and clean the house.

Leroy had fully stepped into his role as step daddy. I had enrolled the girls into daycare and they could stay there until 5:30 p.m. during the week. Leroy had a house in Waco, but he knew I needed him close. The nights he stayed in Hillsboro he would get up to take the girls to daycare so that I could sleep in with the baby. Then he would come back to my apartment to try to get some rest before his shift. He got the girls dropped off from daycare and I wouldn't see him until midnight. We had a system that was working for us.

Leroy's mom, Ms. J, quickly became someone I treated with great reverence. I can't count the number of weekends me and the girls stayed at her home. She let us have her room so that we could be comfortable. Leroy would leave overnight and I would be livid because of it. Waco was his stomping grounds so he stayed in the streets while I was in his mother's bed with the kids. But no matter what happened between him and I, she was always on the side of right. If I was out of line she lovingly got me together. She never judged me because she saw herself in me. When I would spank the girls, she would pull me to the side and say, "You'll break their spirits doing that." I was frustrated. I didn't have much money, her son was stressing me out, and the girls were a lot. She was right though. I had begun to take my frustrations out on them and I was breaking their already fragile spirits. Late at night when the kids were asleep we would sit in her living room and talk about everything. I told her about my life growing up and all the things I had gone through prior to meeting her son. She always said that we lived similar lives. She was once a young mother trying to figure her life out while dealing with certain traumas. She became the voice of reasoning and the perfect example of disciplining with love. Although Leroy's mom was a Jehovah's Witness, I knew what I believed in so I wasn't too bothered by it. I would joke with Leroy about Jehovah's Witnesses not celebrating holidays, but there was nothing that truly concerned me about Ms. J being one.

Regardless of the differences we had, I knew that Ms. J loved me and all of my children. Her heart was pure. We lost our way for a moment. I didn't want her teaching Rhileey about her religion. All she was attempting to do was teach my baby about the bible, but because

I didn't understand it, I snatched Rhileey away from her. Proper communication and understanding on both parts could have saved us almost a year of pain. Most of the pain came from me still having feelings for her son and not being able to process that the relationship was about to be over.

Chapter 7

INDUSTRY BABY

I AM *currently sitting on a cruise ship balcony surrounded by miles of water writing this piece... It's such a serene place. There are 3,000 people on this boat and my happy place is here on this balcony alone. I am so grateful for everything God has done in my life.*

Even though I don't deserve any of it, He still continues to bless me in so many ways.

I get to travel and see things that I never would've imagined.

4 years ago I was shoplifting and scraping up change to buy gas for my little red car. Today I am surrounded by people who have touched so many people with their gifts.

My prayer is that God keeps Me humble and compassionate toward others, it doesn't matter if they are billionaires or living check to check, I will always treat people with respect.

My parents and my mother have always done their best with my siblings and I. I was loved as a child just as much as I am loved today. The time that I spent between my two homes were different in a lot of ways. When I was with my mom we spent a lot of time in church. When I was at my parents' house we went to church, but there were a lot of Sundays when they weren't able to be there. They didn't have 9-5 jobs like most of my friends' parents. Instead my parents traveled around the world touching the lives of many. Up until this chapter, I haven't gone into much detail about my parents being in the entertainment industry, so It is important that I dedicate this entire chapter to them.

For as long as I can remember my parents have been connected in some way to the music business. Before they started their lives together they both were active in the music programs at their schools and church. Most of the stories I heard growing up took place at a musical or in the car on the way home from a musical. Music connected them. One of my favorite stories for them to tell is the first time they kissed. If you haven't heard the story before, they were showing the people that rode with them the "right way" to kiss. The story almost always ends with my dad alleging that my bonus mom skipped all the way to her front door when she was dropped off at home. My second favorite story is how they met. My dad and his friends were part of a singing group. Now the way my dad tells the story is that my bonus mom's best friend bragged to him that she knew someone who would crush all of them on a microphone. My dad was up for the challenge and of course my bonus mom showed up and showed out. It was that small challenge that birthed this power couple. Their friendship blossomed into a secret romance. I can tell you all it's a secret because that was their song. Every time they talked about certain parts of their relationship during this time they burst into song. *Secret Lovers* by Atlantic Starr was my parents' song.

During the time when I first moved in with my father they were touring with Kirk Franklin and The Family. Even though they were away on tour they were still parents to us. While they were on tour we would go back and forth between staying at my grandmother's house and her staying with us at our house. My siblings and I talked to our parents every single day. We gave them updates on our extracurricular activities and they even flew into town to surprise us a few times. We knew when they came home on these surprise pop ups that we were about to spend some quality time together. They'd go to every-one's school to pull us out early. I rarely got early dismissals so when I heard my name being called over the loudspeaker I knew what was going on. The parents were in town. The time they spent away was definitely made up for during these impromptu trips home. We had their undivided attention and I loved that.

My bonus mom had a sister that passed away. So she took on the responsibility of caring for her niece, Sonya, who was only a teenager at the time. Sonya had a sister and a few brothers, but my parents could only afford to take in one child at the time. Sonya became our big sister more so than our cousin. Since Sonya was only 14 when she came to live with us, my grandmother still came to stay with us when my parents had to travel.

By the time Sonya was 18, she was old enough to look after us so we started staying home with her when it was time for the parents to hit the road. She was responsible for making sure we got to school every day, making sure our homework was done, and feeding us. She became such an intentional big sister and there was no limit to the things she did to keep us entertained. One day we spread dish liquid on the floor and turned the dining area into a full skating rink. And Sonya wouldn't just sit back and watch us, she always joined in on the fun. She was a big kid at heart. She always allowed us to play freely, but when it was clean up time we fell right in line. She was very strict about cleaning the mess up. We knew that if we cleaned up the mess she would almost always find another activity for us to do before it was time for bed.

At the age of 22 Sonya moved out of the house. There were a few times in between then when she would run away and come back but this time she was gone for good. At least that's what my young mind thought. Looking back I think the lack of experiencing her teen years caused her to be curious about a lot of things. She had a boyfriend, but also had to look after us when my parents had to work. She was lost.

My time with Sonya was fun, but I always missed my parents when they left. I would sit and wonder what all they had to do on the road.

I mean I knew they sang for a living, but I didn't know the specifics of their job. At the beginning of their career we didn't spend a lot of time with them on the road. While I am sure they wanted us with them every step of the way, they were still establishing themselves as professionals in the industry while parenting us. Being away from our parents for months at a time was hard on each of us in our own way. The sacrifices they were making caused them to miss out on a lot of school activities. Eventually the more they left the easier it became to deal with, but as a young girl I didn't quite understand because my feelings were in the way. There were days when I wished they worked a 9-5 so they could be home with us.

The distance was especially difficult during the holidays. We didn't have many traditions while I was growing up, but the holidays were reserved for family time. If they had to go away for the holidays my bonus mom would pull out the Christmas decorations early so we could still experience that together. Eventually they started to plan trips for us to come out on the road with them. One day they sat us down and said that we would be traveling with them that holiday season to two different cities.

The first city we visited was New York. My parents had to go ahead of us because their work required them to and I had a track meet at the end of the week that we were scheduled to go. My grandmother and her husband would be accompanying us on the trip so we had a lot to prepare for. The weather in New York was cold so we all needed to buy new coats. Burlington Coat Factory was granny's one stop shop for everything. The variety of their coat selections made for an easy shopping trip. We were told to pack and dress in a way that didn't make us look like tourists. We all found these really puffy bubble coats, beanies, gloves, and anything else you can think of that would make us look exactly like tourists. It was like the scene from *Coming to America* when they came out of the store dressed head to toe in the I Love New York attire.

The week we were supposed to leave went by so slowly and I could hardly keep it together because I was filled with so much excitement.

I couldn't focus on the track meet I had coming up because I was too busy thinking about what clothes I wanted to pack for New York. The week leading up to the track meet is when we got all of our things packed. The day of the track meet was supposed to be a breeze. The plan was to have everything ready to go before the day of the meet, so after the meet we would all go home, shower, and prepare for our morning flights.

My grandmother drove us to every extracurricular activity we had, but she didn't drive that well at night. Everything we did almost always was over before nightfall, except for track. The track meet was over around 7:30 p.m. and it hadn't dawned on me that we had a 35-minute drive back home and it was almost dark. On the drive home my granny seemed calm at first, like she had it together. We were all talking about how exciting the trip would be, when all of a sudden she fell quiet.

"Dee, it's too dark," she said.

She was the only one in the car with a driver's license so in my mind I was thinking she has to pull this together so we can at least make it home. The further we got down the road the more her anxiety levels started to rise. The road we had to take was a two-lane country road and there were cars everywhere. Every time one would zip by us she got even more worked up. I slowly talked to her to try to take her mind off of what was happening around us. She didn't realize that we weren't keeping up with the flow of traffic until cars started honking at us and flashing their lights. To avoid any accidents she turned on the hazard lights and we coasted all the way home. As soon as we pulled into the driveway I exhaled. We were safe. The minute we walked in the door we all headed to our rooms to double check that we had everything packed for New York. The moment I got settled in I heard heavy breathing coming from downstairs. She was having a full-blown panic attack and her husband was trying to calm her down. I walked downstairs to see her with a face full of tears leaning on the side of the couch.

"Granny, what should I do?" I asked her.

I didn't know if things were serious enough to call the ambulance, but we made the call anyway. Better safe than sorry is all I was thinking. While we waited for the ambulance I felt like something else should be happening. She was in distress and all I knew to do was talk to her until help arrived. We were really close with our neighbors and they believed in the power of prayer so we went to get them to help out. The grandmother came across the street and said a powerful prayer over my granny. The whole room watched as she slowly started to calm down, and then help arrived. We gave them every piece of information we could think of. We told them what we thought had sparked the attack and then we stepped back to let them go to work. After carefully examining her, they informed us that my granny was having a bad panic attack.

I looked over at my brother and sister and they had a disappointed look on their faces. I think we were all thinking the same thing, but Tia said it out loud.

"Does this mean we can't go to New York?"

I scolded her because it seemed insensitive, but looking back, she had every right to ask a legitimate question. Would we still be able to go to New York? Once the paramedics told us our granny wasn't dying we wanted to know what this meant for our trip. My parents were on the phone during the whole encounter and at the end of the call they assured us that the trip was still on. Granny pulled herself together and we all turned in for the night.

If you have ever been to New York during the holidays then you know it is a magical experience. The moment my foot hit the streets of New York I felt like a tourist. I was a tourist. We did all the things we were told not to do when you visit the city. We walked around with our head glued to the sky admiring the mile high buildings. I was just a little Black girl in this big city for the first time.

When we arrived at our hotel there was a guy being loud outside the hotel doors. My brother had been outside with some of the members of the band when all of a sudden, he ran into the building screaming. My dad instructed all of us to get together and moved us far away from the commotion. There had been some altercation with the guy and David said he had a gun. That was all my dad needed to hear before we were rushed up to our room. "Welcome to New York City," I heard someone say on our way up.

The details of this trip are foggy, but at some point, I remember thinking to myself, "So this is what they do?" Who wouldn't want to travel and visit these beautiful places for a living? It was on that trip that I gained a deeper understanding and respect for what my parents did for work. Their nights were long and their mornings were super early. They would do a show in one city then be in the next before the people in the city opened their eyes the next day. It was truly something to experience. After the concert in New York we boarded the train to Philadelphia for the next show. We were kids who had no clue what tour life was about, but we went with the flow. We all drug our sleepy selves out of bed, got dressed, and headed down to the hotel lobby. My parents were used to traveling so they chuckled at the sight of all of us being passed out in the chairs of the hotel lobby. This was tour life in the music industry. The Philadelphia show was the last stop for us before we were due to go back home. My parents would stay on the road for a few more weeks then come home to be with us.

Kirk Franklin and The Family kick started my parents' careers in the entertainment industry, but the road they would travel was far greater than anything they ever imagined. I wasn't a child who required a lot of material things to be happy, but I enjoyed the blessings their elevation was bringing. I noticed that our homes and cars were upgraded when their finances started to shift. My bonus mom was a stickler for keeping the house stocked with groceries but we started to eat out more often. We weren't name brand kids, but we were teenagers attending public schools. Clothes meant a lot. Even our wardrobe was upgraded. But no matter how much money my parents made they always made sure we remained humble. Their season with Kirk Franklin came to an end and a new thing began.

My dad has always been a character. Long before the world knew who he was he was driving my granny crazy with his antics. One of my favorite things to do is listen to his stories. One day when he was a kid he was messing around in class like class clowns do and he got himself in trouble. His teacher told my granny and she said to him, "You do not get paid to go to school and tell jokes. You are there to learn." Once he became an actor he told her, "Now I get paid to be funny!"

My bonus mom is the most anointed singer I've ever known. Growing up in the industry, I witnessed a lot of great singers, but rarely have I encountered many that are anointed. When she opens her mouth to sing, everything stops. Because I was a child I wasn't privy to the back-room conversations surrounding my parents' careers. They were the epitome of getting it done and making it look good in the process. One day my dad told us he got a role in a stage play and that mama would be going with him because they needed someone with a powerful voice to sing in the plays. There wasn't much excitement on my part because this was another gig to put them on the road. Their new boss was Tyler Perry. The way my mama tells the story is that she made it very clear to Mr. Perry that she was not an actress. Her exact words to him were, "I will sing for you all day long, but I don't act." In return he assured her that he would make an actress out of her before it was all said and done and that is where the characters Mr. Brown and Cora were born.

Their new lives took off very fast.

After one play was done, Mr. Perry had another one already written. There was one play that came across the books that only my bonus mom got the call for. Instead of my dad being intimidated, he prepped her for life on the road and on the stage. Acting came natural to him, but his new role was now stay-at-home dad. Life at home with a stay-at-home dad was a lot different than a mom. When he would send us to the store for a gallon of milk he would send us with like forty bucks. When he first started to do this we would bring him the change back because milk wasn't forty dollars, but eventually we came to the realization that either he doesn't know how much a gallon of milk costs or he gave us extra to keep. Either way we started pocketing the change. Up until this day I still make jokes with them about which parent to ask first. If we asked my mama she was guaranteed to give you the exact amount for whatever you were about to go buy. If we asked my dad he always gave double the amount and didn't expect change.

My dad is a jack of all trades so life as we knew it didn't drastically change. He made sure we still had home cooked meals, he did laundry, and if I was lucky, I could get him to perm my hair. He did it all.

My bonus mom came home from touring with one play and it seemed like the two of them were back on the road again within the next few months. The older I got the less it affected me when they had to leave. I felt like I was built for it, otherwise God wouldn't have placed me in this family. The fans that came out to support them are the reason the plays lasted so long. Every show I went to had a packed house. With each show my parents became more recognizable in the public. We would go out to have family dinners, but it was no longer like before. Now people were coming up to our table asking for their pictures and autographs. It was fun to experience at first until I noticed people had no boundaries. I understand now that they were just excited to see my parents, but as a teen girl who already had to share them with the world, I was selfish with my time. They had a rule when they came to our school games. They didn't take pictures or sign autographs so that they could focus on whoever was on the court or field at the moment. Tia wasn't shy about reinforcing this rule either. One time she stopped mid court in the middle of her basketball game to get my parents' attention because some pushy fan insisted on a picture. "Yall are here to see me, not take pictures," she said. My parents laughed but they respected it. They were becoming superstars and all of our lives were changing rather quickly.

In the middle of their budding success as entertainment moguls my dad started TillyMann Inc., our family business. My bonus mom recorded her first solo album and my father was the brains behind the whole operation. It started with him pouring into my mother. She didn't believe she was a solo artist at first, but my father saw something in her and he pushed her. She didn't sign to any major record labels, everything was done in house. We all worked out of one office for the first couple of years while my dad did the legwork to start building The Mann brand. My first gig with the company started back in 2005. I was fresh out of high school with no plans to go off to college. I was hired as an administrative assistant as well as my bonus mom's travel assistant. The first out of town gig had my nerves all over the place. Most things were done on paper back then so I had a folder that contained the itinerary for the day. I also needed to take my mom's purse because I was her assistant. That was my job. I remember going in to grab her purse and my neat folder of itinerary papers fell to the ground. It was my mom but I was so nervous. I was also young and I had my mind set on living my best life. I didn't really take the job seriously. This became a problem for all of us because my parents were trying to establish themselves as a brand and grow their business, and I wanted to live my life. I wasn't ready to be completely sold out to the family business. My carelessness is the reason I was fired from the job the first time. I was let go around 2007.

My parents went from doing plays to starring in their first sitcom together. *Meet the Browns* is hands down the funniest show they have been in. My favorite episode is when my dad's character got a hold of some marijuana edibles and he thought he was a pimp. The amount of times we quote lines from that episode is enough to make you go watch it all over again. The television shows evolved into films on the big screen. I was still on my hiatus from the family during their transition into films, but I didn't need to be around to know that that was a major accomplishment for them in their career. I was a proud daughter, no matter the distance.

My season in Hillsboro came to an end and in 2013 I decided to move back to the city. It was a bittersweet move for me, because my strongest support system was in Hillsboro. My family there didn't travel for work so they were able to help out with the kids more than my other side of the family. My parents welcomed me back with open arms, but I knew I needed to establish myself. Moving back into their home with three small children was not the ideal situation for me, but it was a sacrifice I was willing to make to improve the way my girls and I were living. The decision to hire me back into the family business came from Tia being let go from the company. I understood that taking the position was going to put a strain on our sister relationship, but I now had children to feed. I was brought back to the company as my parents' assistant. I didn't complain about my position because it felt like a win. I had a job and my parents were the clients. It didn't get any better than that for me at that time in my life.

Things were different this time around. My parents, along with my brother, really structured the company. In addition to music and film they added merchandise to our day to day. I was excited to be a part of the company again because it was the core of the family. I sat down with David to go over all of the things I needed to know about how things were run now. In addition to assisting the parents on the road, I was in charge of all of their travel logistics. Although I hadn't had much experience in administration, it was something I was naturally good at. The world was evolving and our small family business quickly morphed into something great.

I was also put in charge of managing my parents' social media, which is another thing that came natural to me. I was responsible for capturing authentic moments as well as informing the masses of any upcoming events we had. We took a work trip to New York to visit Facebook headquarters and I fell deeper in love with learning how to grow their social media accounts. There I learned how important it was to post and create content according to the analytics. The most important lesson I learned about social media is that people don't like to feel like they are always being sold something. They want to first connect and build an internet relationship with you, then they will support you. I did a lot of research and attempted to apply what I learned not only to the business but also to my life.

When reality television became popular, I never imagined our family would have a show. The shows I watched were pure entertainment and on the edgy side. The Mann Family was definitely entertaining but I was afraid we weren't edgy enough for reality tv. My dad made his boundaries very clear to us and the network executives. We didn't curse each other out in real life so doing that on the show was a no go. There would be no scripted fights or anything that would shed a bad light on our Black family. This was no slight to anyone, but there was already enough of that going on. We wanted our show to be one that the whole family could watch. We did two seasons with the BET network and one season with TV One. The ratings weren't through the roof, but we did well enough to last three seasons. We had our share of ups and downs with the television show, but overall the experience was one for the books. The arguments you saw on the show were real. The love you saw on the show was real. We weren't looking for any more fame, we were just a family sharing our experiences with the hopes that it would bring other families closer together.

At the beginning of 2020 Tyler Perry brought my parents out to do one last stage play, which would also be their first time back on stage together in over 20 years. Tia and I traveled with my parents as their assistants, but Tia had also landed a singing part in the show. She was a part of the group that opened the show and she also did background vocals.

In most of the big cities we went to, it was guaranteed to be a big-name celebrity in the audience that we would most likely get to meet after the show. My favorite after show moment was walking into the meeting room to see Beyonce and Jay Z standing there. They congratulated my parents on a good show and I went in to give Beyonce a hug and she said to me, "I feel like I already know yall from the reality show." My night was made because I am and always will be a part of the Beyhive. That was definitely one of the tour highlights for me. Out of all of the tours I have been on, this one was my favorite. I remember being a kid watching these shows from the dressing room and sneaking on the side of the stage to get a glimpse of my parents. Before the shows would start we would sit backstage and I would just watch all of them. My bonus mom would be warming up her voice as she passed everyone to get to her seat backstage. She had these ginger cut candies that she would pass out to the cast to help speed up the vocal warming process. She was so motherly even in her work environment. My dad has been playing the character of Mr. Brown for years, yet every night he was nervous before going on stage. He paced the floor until we convinced him to take the empty chair next to us. Most of the conversations my parents had before showtime were just them expressing their gratitude. Every night, every city, every show, they would thank God for His faithfulness. They talked about the fact that after all of these years the fans still showed up to see these plays. I took those moments to study. I watched everything and everyone. My parents will forever be a part of history and I was just grateful to be experiencing it as an adult.

During the Madea's Farewell tour my bonus mom got the opportunity to do a few shows with Oprah Winfrey for her health and wellness tour. She was a brand ambassador for Weight Watchers at the time and they wanted her to fly into different cities to share her journey and bless the crowd with her amazing voice. Those days were the days that tested me the most.

Touring was nothing new to me, but our schedule became hectic. My parents would do the play in whatever city it was in at night, then we would hop on a plane to meet The Oprah tour in whatever city it was in that week for an early morning show. When they would reach a certain point in the play, I made my way back to the dressing room to pack all of our things into the car. We had a routine and it was my job to make sure the transitions were smooth. All my parents had to do was walk off stage, change clothes, then get in the car. One week the play was in Los Angeles and the Oprah tour was in New York, so there was no way we would make it to our destination on a commercial flight. They offered to fly my parents and me to these cities on a private jet. This was one of the perks of the job. I had never flown private before.

My first time on a private jet was such a humbling experience. I consider myself to be a humble person, but there was just something about this first. The whole experience is something I'll never forget. My parents paid dues in order for me to experience luxuries of this magnitude. It was important for me to thank my parents on several occasions for bringing me along and giving me the opportunity to experience these things. We leaned on one another heavily during those two tours. The duty of entertaining the masses fell on my parents and the duty to serve fell on me. I stood ten toes down in that position and I'm forever grateful to have experienced it.

During the Oprah Winfrey runs I got to meet a lot of amazing artists and creatives. Oprah greeted me the same way every week that I saw her. Week after week we would sit on the side of the stage while my mom sang her heart out. I didn't fan out because I felt like I was sitting next to an aunt. That is how calm the atmosphere was.

One day after my mom finished tearing down the stage I turned to my left to see someone in a yellow pant suit walking up to us. J. Lo was due to sit down with Oprah for an interview and she came to the stage a few minutes early. She looked up at the screen as my mom walked off and just raised her hands. My mom was a powerhouse and it felt good to see people react to her in that way. It didn't matter what genre of music you sang, when you heard Tamela Mann you stopped to listen. She is truly anointed in that way.

Our last stop with the Oprah and WW tour was Denver, Colorado. Aunt Princess has been a huge fan since as far back as I can remember, so I asked my parents if I could bring her along on the trip. They quickly agreed because it was Aunt Princess. All of the years I have traveled I rarely brought her on the road because she was the person that kept my girls together for me while I traveled, but this was just simply something I couldn't pass up. When would I get another opportunity to experience this with her?

Once Aunt Princess arrived, I documented the whole thing. I pulled my phone out to record every chance I got. The plane ride to Colorado, our hotel room at The Ritz Carlton, and since it was the last show of the tour, Oprah personally stopped in to thank my mom for making time to come out to do her tour. I was only able to capture a quick minute video because I didn't want to be invasive. I knew I had to put my request in for Aunt Princess to take a picture. Oprah said yes with no hesitation and she and Aunt Princess had a moment. She was so kind to my aunt and I knew this was something Aunt Princess would cherish forever. Those are the moments I lived for. The celebrities and private jets were added bonuses, but the smile my aunt had after the trip is something I'll remember forever.

I worked alongside my family for almost 8 years before my season with the company was over. We all had a lane, but we each wore many hats. I've been the tour manager for our family tour, directed my first music video, had my input used for creative projects, and I stepped in wherever I was needed. If the crew needed food and that task was open I stepped in. We covered each other in that way. My time as an assistant will go down as one of the most challenging and fulfilling positions I have been in. The most challenging task was coming to grips with the fact that being an assistant was not a job for flunkies. I can't count how many times I have heard the position of an assistant referred to as a job that most couldn't do. I took pride in being an assistant because at the end of the day, things wouldn't have happened without my contributions. It takes a true servant's heart to work as an assistant because that position requires you to leave your ego at the door. Your attitude and most importantly, your heart, must be in the right place to properly do the job. There is no room for haughtiness because you are the go-to person for almost anything your client needs. My clients just so happened to be my parents so caring for them came naturally.

I had to learn to lean on my support system even more during this time. Aunt Princess and my husband Ace held the house and the girls down while I was out grinding. My aunt sacrificed a lot to be there for me and I'm forever indebted to her for this. There were weeks when I could only pay her with the little money I received from child support and she never complained. When the money was abundant we splurged. I was able to rest at night knowing my girls were safe. Ms. J also helped me find the balance. Her and Aunt Princess had each other's contact information and scheduled visits for Rhileey to go spend time with Ms. J. I didn't have to facilitate it all by myself anymore.

Chapter 8

PLENTY OF FISH

LEROY'S actions made it very clear how he felt about me. I held on for so long because I wanted to be with the father of my child, but it just didn't work out that way. I dated a couple of guys after him. One of the guys was Dominique. We tried to make it work, but his player ways were just too much for me so that faded pretty quick. Next was Dewayne. I learned so many things about myself during our relationship. He helped me on a spiritual and emotional level, but we didn't last either. I take most of the blame for the end of this relationship. I was spoiled and lost.

I was searching for something. I made the mistake of taking everybody home to my family. I say it's a mistake because The Mann Family is a unique group. If you come around us once you will either fall in love or if we don't rock with you, you will know it instantly. My dad and I never got along when it came to my relationships which made things harder for me. After Dewayne and I decided to end things I told myself I wasn't going to take anyone else home. It wasn't because I didn't want to hear what my dad had to say about the people I chose to date, it was because I needed him to respect my decisions whether he agreed with them or not. I was going to date who I wanted to date. When we sat down to have the conversation about him being involved in my personal life things became heated as usual. I flat out told him that if he wanted to be involved in my personal life he was going to have to understand that I would do things a certain way and I didn't need him to protect me from everything.

You see, my father, like most fathers, doesn't believe in letting me bump my own head. The ultimatum I gave him was that I would be open with him about my dating life if he promised not to try to "fix" everything. Sometimes I just wanted to call my dad to vent. I didn't need him to fix things, I just wanted our relationship to be stronger and I still wanted to have the freedom to date and find myself. He married my bonus mom at an early age so he knew nothing about this season of life. His favorite thing to say was that I kept choosing the same men and then in the same breath he would tell me it didn't matter if I came home with the president, he was still going to give me a hard time. How do you move forward with this information? I refused to live my life trying to impress him because nothing I chose to do impressed him. So I decided that I may as well live my own life. On my own terms. With each failed relationship I began to pick up the lessons instead of focusing on the bad decision.

Dating apps were never my thing. They just didn't seem like a legit way to meet people, but here I was, trying to meet someone on a dating app. My profile was created and I just sat there waiting. Waiting for somebody to bite the bait. The first few messages were, "Hey, I'm trying to get to know you. Can you come over tonight?" Come OVER? Sir, you don't even know me like that. This is about to be an interesting journey…

Every single day I had dozens of messages from people that "matched" my vibe. I opened a message from this guy that said, "I love your smile," or something like that and I clicked on his profile. What stood out the most for me is the fact that he was brutally honest and funny. At this time in my life I needed to laugh. I opened the message back and replied to him. We exchanged pleasantries and cracked a few jokes about being on the dating site and how bogus my bio was. According to my bio my perfect date night included drinks and I was not a drinker at all.

I needed something new in my life. I was about to hit a milestone age and I just started to feel different. Let's see where this goes.

Our conversations through text were light. We would send each other songs to listen to and funny memes from Instagram. We still hadn't met each other in person so I decided to give him a call because I felt like it was time to meet up. I didn't know how to just come out and say, "hey, I want to come over and spend some time with you," but the reason I could not say those words is because I knew what my plan was. I had reverted back to early 20s Porcia. I was going to jump into something with this new guy, Ace, to get Dewayne out of my system. The worst thing I could've done. After a 2-hour conversation and me dropping hints that I had no plans that night, Ace invited me over.

I hopped in the shower and threw on some clothes. I was not into makeup and dressing all fancy. Black tights, an oversized shirt, and some slides was the outfit I chose to go meet my future husband in. When I pulled up to his house I saw two cars in the driveway and automatically panicked. Dude tryna set me up. I took a photo of both of the license plates and texted them along with the address to my cousin Tonya. I told her if anything was to happen to me this is who did it and this was his address. She didn't ask any questions, she just said, "I got you."

I walked up to what looked to be a townhome and I rang the bell. I heard a dog bark then the door swung open. Ace was about 6'2, brown skin, and he had a full beard. As I was scanning him over he was looking over my shoulder as if somebody was supposed to be behind me. I walked into what was clearly a bachelor pad. Pit-bull laying by the back door. His living room table was full of papers and cups and just junk. Next to the pile of junk was a small pistol. Surprisingly I wasn't afraid. I actually felt safe.

He gripped me up and gave me the longest hug.

"You want a drink?"

"No, I'm ok," I said. "I'll take some food though because I'm starving." I have never been the type of woman that didn't eat in front of men. I actually had to make sure I wasn't hungry because hangry Porcia is not the best person to be around. We stopped in his living room because that's where he had been watching tv.

I was already aware that he had a 13-year-old daughter, but I thought it was too soon to ask about her whereabouts.

The communication between us was effortless because it was new. I knew before I left my house that I wanted to stay the night with him. I can't even remember what we watched, I just remember thinking about Dewayne. Why did I even come here knowing I wasn't fully healed from my last relationship? I needed to be touched, bad.

I looked at my phone and noticed how late it was. I wasn't ready to leave yet so I leaned in a little closer to him. I noticed that he was a little awkward and didn't pick up on any hint that I was giving him. As the night went on I eventually found myself laying on this man's lap pouring my heart out to him. He just listened to me. Not only did I need to be heard I needed to be touched. BAD. I had officially set the wrong foundation for whatever this was about to become. We had sex that night and it was BOMB! As soon as he went into the restroom I just laid there staring at the ceiling. What did I just do?

As a young girl I would always say that I was going to wait until I was married to have sex and that I would never have casual meaningless sex with a man. Oh to be young again. I don't know about other women, but I go into situations with the intention of just giving myself to a person whole heartedly. Time and time again each one of those situations failed because I was just lonely and seeking companionship. Outside of Maddison's father and my high school love, I have never been friends with the men I dealt with before having a relationship with them. I know from experience that it is important to build that foundation as a friend before entering into any type of physical relationship with another person. Once the sex gets old and things start to look like they are going downhill, y'all will have that friendship to fall back on and try to work at mending the relationship if possible.

The "honeymoon" phase served its purpose for me. Ace was such a gentleman. Before our first date he texted me and said, "hey, Friday we're going out. It's real chill so you don't have to dress all fancy." Food is the way to my heart. I'm not a real barbecue girl, but there were two things I knew: I was STARVING and I could not get hangry on our first date. I loved the fact that he planned something out for us to do. He took the time to romance me, he learned the way to my heart and he planned dates around that.

Ace was very intentional with the way he protected me. He was a natural protector. It was genuine. Anything I asked of him he made efforts to change so how could I not fall in love with this man? If I was lacking money to pay a bill all I would have to do was ask him.

When Ace and I first started dating I wasn't aware of his PTSD. We had so many conversations about him being in the army and I cracked a joke saying he was "crazy" because that's what I'd heard about people with PTSD. He didn't find that funny at all and if you know Ace you know that he doesn't mind telling you what he feels. "I am not crazy, but I do have PTSD and I don't think that shit is funny." I felt like an idiot. No, an uneducated idiot. I offended him and I didn't know what PTSD was! "Imagine being trained for 3 years to hurt, hurt, hurt and after you're out no one tells you how to turn the switch off," he said. I'd never thought about it that way.

Ace was stationed in Colorado Springs when he became a "single father." His mom helped out with his daughter while he was in basic training, but after that he sent for her to come live with him. "My daughter saved my life and helped me cope with PTSD." The moments when he wanted to get lost in his thoughts his daughter made him snap out of it. He told me so many stories, but the ones that stuck out are the beginning phases that took place after basic training. "What should I feed her? Should I ask her if she's hungry? Am I cut out for this?" Ace has always been a figure-it-out kind of person and that's exactly what he did. He said, "I looked at her and said 'aight, let's do it'." Everything wasn't always a cake walk during this time. He told me a hair story that tickled me and made my heart smile at the same time. The neighbor that usually helped him comb her hair wasn't available one day so he figured he would just hook up the curling iron and make it happen. Let's just say after he tried and failed he took her to get her hair braided and kept it like that.

There are two main things that you need to know if you're in a relationship with someone who suffers from PTSD. You did not cause it and most importantly you can NOT fix them. Prayer, love, and support is all you can offer! Also, you don't need to treat them as if they are handicapped. After being checked in a major way I started to do my research. I wasn't scared of Ace, I was intrigued by him. I needed to know what triggers he had, what was off limits. I wanted to know it all. The first trigger I learned about was different sounds. If you own an iPhone then you know the classic alarm sound. That was my ring tone and my alarm to wake me up. Ace spent the night at my house one night and in the middle of the night I got a phone call. He sat straight up in the bed and b-lined to the bathroom and pulled the shower curtain back. I jumped right up and went right after him because I didn't know what was going on. I turned the corner to find him standing beside the shower with his face buried in his hands. "What happened???" I was so confused. He said, "that sound." Huh? "That sound is the sound for an incoming bomb," he said. I felt so horrible. I made the adjustment and changed my ringtone right away. We got back in bed and I just held him. My goal was to make sure that he never felt alone again.

The weekends were ours. One particular weekend Ace started hinting at not being able to hang out the whole weekend, which was fine because I was going to be with my parents doing family stuff. He said that he was driving a family friend to Waco for a funeral. It didn't sound right to me, but I didn't want to come off as pushy because we were still kind of new. I told him it was all good and we could just link up when he got back in town. Of course I didn't hear from him the whole day. I texted him and my messages went unanswered. I finally got a text around 11:30 at night saying, "Hey, babe. I just made it back home and my phone has been dead all day." My gut told me it was some bullshit, but he had some good dick so I noted that shit in my memory.

I replied, "It's all good. Glad you are safe."

The next day I went to see him and in addition to his cars there was a little gold SUV parked in front of the mailbox. I was curious but I didn't say anything. I waited for him to tell me whose car that was. Normally when I would visit I spent the night, but this time he said, "I have to pick my homeboy up from the airport in the morning. That's his car outside."

"Oh, ok, that's cool. Ima head home in a little bit since you have to get up early," I said.

I didn't think anything of it because we were connecting in a way and we were open and honest with each other, so there was no reason for him to lie.

Every time we hung out we had sex. This time was no different. Before heading home I snapped a quick selfie with his headboard and his Painting with a Twist photos in the back, posted to Snapchat, and then I was on the road.

A few days later I was at my parents' house and my Instagram direct message was booming. I didn't typically get many messages so when I saw that I got 3 messages with photos attached, I was like "what the hell?"

I opened the first picture and it was this girl and Ace making silly faces.

Next picture, Ace and the same girl on his bed.

The last photo was a silly face photo of them in the same gold SUV I saw parked in front of his house the night he told me he had to go pick up his homeboy from the airport.

Her message read, "I just made love to him in that bed a few nights ago."

I assume she saw my photo somehow and noticed the pictures in my background. "He is a good man, but he is not being honest with you." She proceeded to tell me that he drove her and her sons to Waco a couple of weeks ago to somebody's funeral. My heart DROPPED. I knew he was full of it.

I instantly called him.

"Hello?"

"You know somebody named Erica?" I asked.

"Yeah, that's my home girl," he lied.

"Well, according to these pictures and this message y'all are more than friends." I screenshot the messages and sent them to him. "Why did you lie?"

"She is crazy, we aren't in a relationship."

Why do men give you good penis then turn around and call you crazy in the same breath? Just say you got caught up.

I started to snap, but I caught myself. "Well, can you keep her crazy ass away from me," I said sarcastically. "And I thought we agreed to cut off other people?"

"You want me to block her," he asked.

"YES. YOU WERE SUPPOSED TO ALREADY BEEN BLOCKED THESE HOES."

He sent me a screenshot of him blocking her and that was the end of it.

Why did I let it go that easy? That was the first day that he slowly started to chip away at our trust. But my heart was hungry, so all of the lies he fed me, I ate them up without thinking.

Before I decided to introduce the girls to Ace I had to have a few talks with myself. Dating with daughters is a whole different ball game. You have to be very observant and intuitive. We have had so many talks about their boundaries and they are comfortable with coming to me if they feel something isn't right. I have no shame when it comes to asking them if they have been touched inappropriately. They know not to sit in any man's lap and if they feel uncomfortable they immediately let me know. When they were smaller and couldn't communicate certain things to me I didn't let them go around very many people, only a couple of close family members that I REALLY trusted. Call me paranoid, but I would rather be safe than sorry. I am going to be as transparent with y'all as possible. I was dating a guy before Ace and I introduced the girls to him. After we broke up one of my daughters said, "mama, if you get another boyfriend, please don't break up with him because we want a house with a mom and a dad." What was I supposed to say? She was right. So this time I wanted to be sure that whatever man I brought around them had a good chance of staying around.

Going back to my initial point of when you should introduce the man you're dating to your daughters, the answer is *when you feel comfortable!* I waited for a little while before I introduced Ace to the girls. The initial meeting was a little awkward for me because my girls are clowns. They were making kissy faces behind his back and then turned around and asked me a thousand questions about him.

The first time I decided to leave the girls with Ace for the weekend was very hard for me. Aunt Princess normally kept the girls when I traveled for work, but she was busy this particular weekend. Ace knew how I felt about my girls so he didn't take it personally when I expressed how nervous I was. They were old enough to tell me if they felt uncomfortable about anything and they didn't hold back. His daughter (now my bonus daughter) that has been living with him since she was a toddler was there to assist him with all the girly stuff they needed. He could have easily been offended by how nervous I was, but he was so understanding and reassuring. All of the girls had iPads and I was able to FaceTime them anytime I needed to. The whole time (all of two days) I was gone I ran every scenario through my head. I couldn't wait to get to the girls to ask them how things went. When I got back they told me they had the best time and they bragged about his cooking and said he cooked better than I did. I asked if they felt uncomfortable and they said, "no, mama, we were fine." I won't lie and say that after that first time it was smooth sailing. It still took me a little time to adjust, but now that we were in the same house when I traveled for work, the girls stayed home with him. I didn't expect him to do everything the way that I did, but he was willing to learn and that's what mattered.

Now buckle up, because the next few months are going to fly by.

Ace and I decided that moving in together would be the most convenient thing. It would certainly make both of our lives easier financially. I was overwhelmed by the move in the beginning because I was afraid of change because it would force me out of my comfort zone, but I was willing to try.

The vibe in our new little family house was something I had wanted for a long time. We kicked it for those first few months. Ace sat on the end of the couch and I laid on him while we talked and laughed so many nights. I decided that I wanted to be with him and I wanted to do it the "right" way since I had gotten it wrong so many times. I came across a video of Priscilla Shirer talking about abstaining from sex. Ace and I had crossed that threshold a long time ago, but it was something Priscilla said in her video that caught my attention. I was tired of getting it wrong and if this was a step in the right direction then that's where I needed to be. After talking myself up to it I went to him and told him I wanted to become celibate. Now Ace is a Scorpio man and if you know anything about Scorpio men you know that sex plays a MAJOR part in how the relationship will go. He was PISSED at me, but it was because it was out of the blue. Understandably too, because here we are just moving in together and our life seemed great and suddenly I applied pressure. But I felt like if I was worth it to him then he would agree, and he did. We slipped up several times trying to do things the right way, but we just started over. I thought this would make us lean onto each other more, but after a while, Ace wasn't having any of that. He slept on the couch most of the time, which made me feel uncomfortable until he broke it down for me. He told me that I was worth doing this, but every day wasn't going to go the way I thought it should and he was right. This was new for both of us and he had to process it his own way.

One weekend in the summer, Ace planned a "small" house warming party so that our friends and family could come together and have a good time. In my mind it would just be a few family members, my friends, his friends, and our kids. I would get enough food to feed about 30 people and that was it. I should've known something was up when he told me his uncle who "just loves to travel" was going to fly in for the party. Seven o'clock approached so I hopped in the shower and threw on some ripped jeans, a lil crop top, and some slides. Threw my hair in a ponytail and people started showing up. AND THEY KEPT COMING!!!! I pulled Ace to the side and was like, "um, why did you invite all these people and not tell me?? I didn't get enough food!!" He just told me to relax and asked his mom to pick up some stuff on her way over so that made me feel a little better. Our families were getting along great, everyone was running through the food, and I was about ready to wrap things up. I'm not that good of a host because after so long I will run out of things to talk about (horrible)! So I started washing dishes, secretly hoping that people would get the hint: THERE IS NO MORE FOOD! GO HOME!

There were people everywhere. The women were inside and the men outside. I noticed everyone coming back inside the house so I gave Ace the, "Bruh, ain't no mo food, and I'm all out of entertainment face." I was drying off the cutting board when he grabbed me and said, "Let's thank everyone for coming and getting along and all that good stuff."

When we got in the family room he started this long speech and in my head I was like, "Oh, lord, he's been drinking and he is about to talk these people's heads off!" So I interrupted him and let everyone know that my speech would NOT be that long and I thanked them for coming. Then I noticed that everyone had their cell phones out?? I immediately started to get nervous. First of all, I'm claustrophobic AND his speech started going from thanking everyone to things like, "I thank God I met this woman. When I first met her she was broken, we were both broken." He went on to say, "I thank God that I've been broken enough to understand her shattered pieces…" I just remember his brother standing right behind us high fiving him and hugging him. The words that made my heart melt were, "I can't go another day without asking this woman to marry me!!" The whole living room went CRAZY and I pulled my shirt up over my face to hide the tears. Inside I was thinking, "this is what you deserve! This is the moment you have been waiting for. All those nights you soaked your pillow with tears, all of the doubt and fear of your heart being handed to someone and it getting shattered…it's over!" I said yes.

But just as quickly as the excitement came in, so did the worry. It seemed like the minute I accepted Ace's proposal all of the reservations I had about us as a couple flooded my mind. We were not ready for marriage, but he took a leap by asking me, so I took the same leap of trusting him.

JOURNAL ENTRY

It took me one day and two stores to find my wedding dress!! Before we started dress shopping I already made up in my mind that I was going to find the dress that day. We went to the first store and the lady had all these dresses picked out. 3…2…1 GO! I tried on the first dress and it was SOOOO PRETTY. In my mind that was it, I like it and let's go. Wrong. "Try on more," they said. I tried on big dresses, tight dresses, white dresses, super long dresses, I mean GAH-LEE! With no luck at the first store we landed at this beautiful bridal store and before we got out the car I was like, "Yeah, if I don't find it in here I'm done looking for today."

The second store was a bit smaller, but the dresses were stunning. I knew I wanted a simple dress that I could be comfortable in but still beautiful. I wanted it to be mermaid fitted with long sleeves.

There was this dress on a mannequin that I passed by but didn't pay attention to. I glanced at it and followed the lady in the back to get started. *My parents, my mom, Ace's mom, my best friend Jaz, Tonya, and Tia were all with me on this day, so this time they all picked out a dress they wanted me to try on. So I started trying on everybody's dress and then Jaz was like, "just try this last one on." It was the dress that I walked by. On the Mannequin it was just ok, but when I put it on...I KNEW INSTANTLY!!! Everyone was still outside of the dressing room, but when I looked at myself in the mirror I started to tear up. "You are a bride, a BEAUTIFUL bride at that." I had a little moment to myself before pulling back the curtain. I took a little walk in front of everyone and they Ooo'd and Aww'd. I made sure I could stand up and sit down comfortably and twerk a lil sum (because duh)...I SAID YES TO THE DRESS (and I did it in one day).*

Chapter 9

TIL HARDSHIPS
DO US PART

OFTENTIMES we hear people talk about the beautiful parts of marriage, but it's rare to hear about the struggles that come with it. I was the product of a blended family so the struggles were familiar to me. The difference this time was that I had stepped into a different role. I wasn't a child trying to fit into a new family, I was now one of the people responsible for facilitating these transitions.

I never thought I would see myself with three children, let alone three daughters. Let's add a teenager, two bonus sons, one of whom I never met because of grown-up foolishness, and a man into the equation. I felt SUPER lost and my emotions were all over the place.

I was in the middle of planning a wedding when Ace and I had a huge argument; he had been on the couch all week. When we had arguments we would go days without saying one word to each other. This time it got so bad that my daughter came to me and asked if the wedding was off. She could feel the tension. The whole vibe of the house was just off. A month before the wedding we wanted to call it off. The pressure that had built up from being celibate mixed with the new responsibilities were too much for us. We were way in over our heads, but one thing was clear for both of us, we had each other's back no matter what. At the beginning of this relationship we said forever through whatever and a month before our wedding was no different. We were going to push through.

The days leading up to the wedding were intense. I had to pick my dress up, make sure the children's clothes were together, and mentally prepare myself. I didn't want to rush through this time. I needed to take it all in.

Nerra and Rae drove in the night before the wedding to be with me. I thought I wanted the night before to just be alone, but once they came I realized that their energy was exactly what I needed. I needed laughs and some good conversation.

The "big" day for me started out so perfect. We woke up, fed the kids breakfast, packed the car with all of our things, then headed out. When we made it to the venue I saw everyone running around setting the scene for this beautiful day. There were white chairs to the left and right and the aisle was lined with red roses down each side. The grounds behind the altar were picturesque. The ceremony was about to be beautiful. I wanted to help with the set-up. There was no way I could go up to my room and sit while everyone was doing everything.

I walked into the bridal suite to see my sister-in-law steaming the bridesmaids' robes and a couple of my bridesmaids were already getting their makeup done. I made my way around the room with my anxious energy. My sisters were trying to keep me occupied but I couldn't sit still. My initial thought was for the bridal suite to be peaceful and quiet because I needed to "focus" and reflect. I didn't want there to be any chaos. I am so glad my bridesmaids didn't listen to me because I would have gone CRAZY sitting in that room all by myself. They had music playing, the kids were running around playing, and we had people in and out right up until it was time for me to walk out. I made sure I looked at everything taking place in the room while I was getting all dolled up. I wanted to live in those moments.

I looked in one corner and my daughter was painting my grandma's nails, then I looked back around later to see she was brushing my mom's hair.

As the day went on I noticed more and more clouds rolling in and the sun was totally covered. I was so bummed about the weather because the ceremony was supposed to take place outside and then everyone would come inside for the reception. My mom finally came into the bridal suite and asked me if I wanted to go ahead and move everything inside because the rain was coming in. I checked the weather app on my phone and saw that it was a 90% chance of rain so I asked her to move everything inside. All of the moving was taking place as I was finishing my makeup, seconds before I put on my dress. I almost started crying, but then I had to tell myself that it wasn't about the weather or the decorations. This moment was bigger than the weather. My dad was the first person to see me before I got ready to walk down the aisle. I stood at the top of the stairs anxious because they were taking too long to start. Had the rain stopped? Did they get everything moved inside? I couldn't wait any longer. Before we made it to the door my dad stopped and asked me if I was sure that this was what I wanted. This was a fine time to ask considering everyone was standing on the other side of the doors with their phones up waiting for us. I thought I was ready…

The feeling I had just before those doors opened is one that I can't put into words, but I will try. I thanked God for allowing me the honor of being someone's wife and I asked Him to guide me the whole way. With each step I took I imagined myself stepping over every bad decision, every guy who ever made me feel like I wasn't good enough, every person in my life who held my past against me, and every tear I shed. I walked all the way past my past! I looked up about halfway down the aisle to find Ace's eyes. I didn't expect to see him crying because that's not what he does. I looked up and saw him and his groomsmen smiling from ear to ear.

Ace, his family, and friends are free spirited people. They have a CRAZY sense of humor, but the one thing I loved about their presence at the wedding was the genuine love they had for us. All that mattered to them was the fact that we were happy. They didn't care who was looking or who did what. They danced ALL NIGHT long! We both decided to write our vows and read them during the ceremony. I am so happy we recorded the ceremony because my anxiety apparently makes me deaf. I could see everyone, but I couldn't hear that well. Ace began his vows and the tears started up again. Someone on his side screamed "Dilly Dilly" in the middle of Ace saying his vows and Ace repeated it. All of the groomsmen joined in and it became a thing. I was just glad the focus shifted off of me for a moment and Ace knew that. My parents on the other hand were hot. They didn't think he took the vows seriously which, to them, obviously meant he wouldn't take our new life seriously. But they didn't know him the way I did. I was someone's number 1. That is something I have NEVER been before and honestly it felt good to love someone and be loved back. I was his WIFE!!

Ace and I didn't go on a real honeymoon because it was time to get back to work. The Stellar Awards took place in Las Vegas that year and since we were newly married, Ace would come to work with me and we would try to get some honeymoon time in. My parents and I hadn't spoken about their behavior at our wedding and it bothered me. The whole family was going to Vegas and I thought we needed to talk before we had to spend the entire weekend together. I was not supposed to be dealing with this type of shit days after my wedding. The day before we went to sit down with my family, Ace and I sat down to watch our wedding video and I was disgusted at the faces my parents were making. He said "Porcia, look at all these other people that are genuinely happy for us. Focus on that." He was absolutely right, but I couldn't let it go.

We pulled up to my parents' house and Ace stopped me before getting out of the car. He said, "I need you to understand that I am not for everybody. Your parents may never like me and I'm ok with that. I just need you to be. I have a family that loves me and that's enough for me. As long as you and these girls are taken care of, I'm good." I appreciated that from him, but I needed to get some stuff off my chest. We started the "meeting" off by letting everybody express their concerns. My parents' main concern was the fact that they felt like Ace didn't take the vows seriously enough for them. I tried time after time to explain to them why what happened during Ace's vows didn't affect me and they needed to let it go. It made the moment better for me actually because it allowed me to breathe. Even if they did have concerns, my wedding was not the place to express them. Ace was the same person every time they saw him so I don't know what they expected.

We had some very heated exchanges that day, but we ended it with mutual respect. My Dad made it very clear that although he didn't agree with the way things went, he respects the sanctity of marriage. Ace was my husband and if I was happy that's all that mattered. That's all I wanted. My life didn't feel like a dream, but I was comfortable. I was with the man I wanted to spend the rest of my life with, the handful of friends I had brought so much joy to my life, and my daughters were happy and healthy.

At the end of the summer Ace and I drove to Florida to celebrate our friends Chris and Fiona's nuptials. Their love story is one of my favorite stories, so to be a part of their celebration was special to me. The wedding would take place on the beach in front of a few family members and friends and the reception would be in the backyard of the beach house. Before we left to go on the trip, Fiona and I sat down and had a conversation. She let me know that her and Ace's ex-girlfriend were still friends. She proceeded to tell me that she would also be joining the wedding festivities down in Florida, but there was to be no drama because Fiona didn't play that. I was still an outsider to this circle so I had my guard up, but I kept it cute. The only person that really owed me anything was my husband. As long as he kept it respectful then all would be well. I had to put my big girl panties on because the weekend wasn't about me.

During Chris and Fiona's wedding reception we danced into the night. Ace tried to keep up with our nieces and nephews on the dance floor, but his age got the best of him. He made his way back to the table to sit down every once in a while, until he heard another song he wanted to dance to. I didn't dance too much because I couldn't stay away from the food table. I was 6 months into my new marriage and I was packing on the pounds. I had gained about 25 pounds of "happy weight" and it showed. I also didn't want to come off like I was trying to show off because his ex-girlfriend was there. I wasn't too worried about him and his ex being sneaky, but I kept my eyes open. There was no funny business that night, but that *was* the night Ace saw something that he wanted to rekindle. The next 6 months were about to shake my world and I didn't even see it coming.

Traveling for work was already hard because I had to be away from my family so much. I was with my parents, but my newly blended family was falling apart and I felt it. I needed to be home but I also had to work. Ace and I were coming up on our one-year anniversary and of course I would be working during that time.

I had a few extra days left at home and I wanted to make sure I gave everyone their time and attention. The girls needed me and so did Ace. The night before I left to go out of town was supposed to be quality time for us. After I got back from Hillsboro picking Aunt Princess up, we would head home and he would have my undivided attention once he made it home from work. At least that was the plan.

Aunt Princess and I pulled into the driveway of our home and my Instagram notification went off.

I opened my phone and saw that I had 3 messages.

I opened the first message and it was from Ace's ex-girlfriend. Before I scrolled down to read the other messages my mind instantly went back to Chris and Fiona's wedding. I knew full well what storm I was about to walk into.

Her message said, "Give me a call," and attached was a naked picture of my husband standing in our bathroom looking stupid.

I got her number and called her immediately.

"Hello," I said.

"Hey, I feel like we need to talk," she said.

"What's up?" My plan was to listen and gather the evidence because I was about to spaz on Ace. 1 week before our one-year wedding anniversary you pull this shit on me?

"Me and Ace have been sleeping together for about 5 months now," she said.

My heart dropped.

"He has been telling me that he's going to file for divorce March 1st and last night he started acting differently. He's been doing this to me on and off for years and I'm tired of it," she said. "These deadlines are coming up and he ain't acting the same."

I don't know what she expected me to say. She's literally calling me to get clarity about why my husband was acting funny with her.

"Interesting," I said.

"We have been planning a life together and now he's telling me he wants to make things work with his wife," she said. "If I have to be hurt and miserable then so does he. He's been blowing me up asking me not to expose him."

"Wait, you already talked to him about this," I asked.

I had been talking to him all day long and he hadn't mentioned to me that his side chick was about to blow his shit up.

"Yes. Last night I was going to come to your house because he wasn't taking my calls," she said.

"He came over here last Tuesday to drop my birthday gifts off and for Valentine's Day he got me a full Harry Potter set because I LOVE Harry Potter."

I started boiling. Valentine's Day went straight to the top of my least favorite holidays list. They had sex the day after Valentine's day and I knew it. I remembered because that night he made up a dumb ass excuse to get off the phone. He told me he was going over to his brother's house to pick up some baked potatoes for their catering business. After we hung up I called him right back to see if he would pick up and got no answer. I knew something was up. When he called me back the next morning he was happy and singing and shit. Did he think that I was that naive? The only time his dumb ass expressed any type of happiness was after he got his dick wet. I couldn't prove it that day so I played it cool. I let him give me the bullshit excuse of his phone dying and I kept it cool. She had just confirmed everything for me.

"How do you know where we live?" I asked her.

"I saw your address on something," she answered.

"Have you been to my house?"

"No, I would never." She said.

I asked her if this started before or after we saw her at Chris and Fiona's wedding and she told me it started after. I knew it. She went on to tell me that it started out with them just catching up. Ace and I were having issues in our marriage and he turned to her for "comfort."

"The only reason I fell for him again is because he pursued me hard," she said. "He popped up where I was and passed messages through mutual friends to get to me."

I felt sick.

The rest of the conversation was a blur for me. I couldn't feel anything. Pain slowly started to become a familiar feeling for me with Ace.

As soon as I hung up with her I called him back.

"Hello," he answered cautiously.

"I just talked to your side bitch," I said angrily.

"I'm headed home and I'll explain everything to you," he said.

That was the longest 15 minutes.

All I could think about was the fact that he was pillow talking with this bitch about me and all of our personal business.

He walked in the door and he didn't even deny it. He just started talking. I didn't care about how forthcoming he was now, because he should have just come to talk to me. Everything I had been begging him for he freely gave to the next woman. Fuck his apologies and explanations.

"You were on the road and we weren't having sex as much. She doesn't mean anything to me."

I was silent. Hurt turned into rage and I needed to get away from him.

"I'm sorry, babe," he said this over and over, but for some reason it wasn't registering. All I could really focus on was the fact that he ran my name through the mud with the same bitch he told me not to worry about.

I stood on the side of the bed and just looked at him disgusted.

"What can I do to make it right?" he asked. He got down on both knees and grabbed my hands, but I didn't want to hear him. How did he let this happen? I was a new wife just like he was a new husband so I didn't want to hear the bullshit excuses. He could have talked to me.

"Do you love her?" I asked.

"No. I've never told her I loved her, ever," he said.

All I could do was cry.

"Why am I going through this shit all over again," I thought to myself. I had convinced myself that I deserved a love that sometimes hurts.

I should've left him that day but I didn't want to. It wasn't that I couldn't, I wasn't ready to. When I got married I meant it when I said forever through whatever. Once the dust settled I had to have uncomfortable conversations with myself. Sex had become an issue with us, but we pushed right past that red flag. I knew I wasn't being satisfied on a romantic level, but I decided to stay anyway. I was on the road, but I rarely sent him sexy pictures because I wasn't comfortable with my body. I gained damn near 30 pounds and I really didn't like what I saw when I looked in the mirror. He never pressured me about gaining weight, hell I actually think he loved the extra cushion, it was just me. I had a lot to learn about being someone's wife. Being a wife was much more than I thought I knew. Our lives got busy with work and kids and something kept telling me that it was too early in a marriage to be at this point. We were still supposed to be in the honeymoon phase. Why didn't we just end it there?

Houston, Texas was the next stop for the tour and I was ready to get back on the road. The road was my escape from reality. I knew I wasn't going to leave Ace, but I told him that the trust was shattered and it would take me a while to forgive this. I would never forget it because of the way it made me feel, but I had to forgive him. After all, that's what marriage is about, right? I forgave him, but I had revenge on my mind. I didn't have a revenge plan in mind, I just knew I wanted to hurt him. Pain will make you think some crazy things. I should've stopped everything and stayed home to fix my marriage, but duty called. Before he cheated I wouldn't even entertain a conversation with anyone. I turned everyone away. I was tried daily, but I didn't want anyone else. Up until now.

I didn't trust that he was totally done with her, but I didn't want to live my life being suspicious. The old boyfriends and homeboys that I had blocked in my phone were unblocked. If he wanted to play then I would show him how to do it.

To "make up" for everything that happened Ace surprised me and drove down to Houston to be with me for our anniversary. I was so mad at him, but I was happy he was there. After all, this was our one-year wedding anniversary and I wanted to be with him. We talked for hours in that hotel room. Tia told me she would hold the parents down so that I could spend the day with Ace. We didn't have any real plans, we just kicked it. It reminded me of the beginning of our relationship. All we did was eat, talk, and have sex. We talked about what our lives would be like from this point. In my heart I wanted to forgive him and forget about it all, but I wasn't built that way. I asked him to be patient with me while the trust was repaired. I was upfront about having bad days. Every time he said he was going somewhere I second guessed it. I didn't always speak on it, but in the back of my mind I felt like everything he said was a lie. He told me that it didn't matter how long it took, he wasn't going anywhere.

This time when I went back on the road, I would find myself a side boo. Men are so easy, it took no time to find a victim. All you have to do is smile and stroke their ego and you're in. The man I chose had a woman and he knew I was married. The boundaries were very clear. We didn't link up while other people were around, we had to be strategic with this mess we were creating. I didn't even tell Tia what I was doing because it really was only my business.

Sex wasn't an option for me because I wasn't that bold, yet. I wanted to jump out there, but not too far. I looked forward to his good morning text messages because it was new. He was my escape from reality. We didn't share any real responsibilities or attachments so it was easy to get lost in him. When we were on the road we communicated all day every day, and when I went home he knew not to contact me. We had an understanding. I did my dirt thinking it would fill the void and take away the pain I felt from Ace's cheating. Two wrongs don't make a right, but It felt good to escape my reality for a while. I was emotionally starving and my travel boo fed me.

That temporary high wouldn't last long though and I knew it. I ended the fling after the tour was over because it was time to go home and face the noise. It was fun, but the attention I was getting from the man on the road, I wanted from my husband. When I got home I decided not to tell Ace about my emotional affair. It was a selfish thing to do, but that was my truth. I sat with the secret for a very long time because I was dead wrong. He is aware now because I wouldn't dare write a book about it and not tell the man I married. My thought process was this: It wasn't like I was having sex with the dude, I was just passing time. I did so much talking about Ace not being ready to be a husband that I didn't even realize I was failing as a wife in the process. I no longer made my marriage a top priority. I had focused most of my time and attention on building this temporary thing with this other man when I should have been at home fighting to keep my marriage together. The "revenge" was meant to hurt Ace, but it caused me to see myself. I was just as responsible for our failing marriage.

The attempts to fix our marriage seemed to be working at first. The first thing we tried to repair was the trust that had been shattered. Next, we focused on dating one another again. We designated Friday nights for that.

Occasionally we would have to drag the kids out with us for date night, but most of the time it was just us. I didn't like to go out because I spent most of my time away from home already, but I was willing to do anything to make this marriage work. Our home was my sanctuary. I didn't need a crowd, I genuinely enjoyed just being around him. His off days were my favorite because we bonded the most on those days. Food has always been the way to my heart and he never slacked in that area. Most of his days off I cooked dinner, but he also had a deep love for cooking. It wasn't a task for him because he enjoyed doing it. If he got a new seasoning in the mail he was happy about it. He would whip up these delicious country style meals, fix my plate, and then let me relax. Even if I insisted on cooking he would just put his hand up and say, "I got it." His way of relaxing included things like taking his guns apart to clean them and vacuum sealing all of the meats he had smoked the day before. Those things are what relaxed him.

The garage was our go-to spot. He fixed his drinks and I smoked my herbs and we just kicked it. We prioritized one another and I believe that's what got us through the bad days.

On occasions when we felt like it we did dress up and go out. We both hated the idea of putting on "fancy" clothes, but we knew it was necessary for us to do it every now and then. We didn't do anything too far left, but the more I think about it, maybe we should have. Did he want to be more spontaneous and he just didn't tell me? We didn't have a lot of money so the things we could do were limited. Our life didn't seem boring, but could we have added more spice to it? These are all of the things I didn't think about until life happened.

Although I had forgiven Ace for the infidelity, I still had major trust issues. For months straight I would wake up in the middle of the night to check his phone records. Even when I would tell myself that checking phone records was unhealthy, I still had to look. If I found a random number I would call to see who he had been talking to. I became obsessed with searching for dirt, more than actually getting to the root of my trust issues. On the outside it seemed like we were making progress, but in reality, I was secretly tearing down everything we were trying to rebuild.

JOURNAL ENTRY
NOVEMBER 2021

I will never beat myself up for making the decision to get married. Although it was a rough journey I wouldn't trade in those lessons for anything. The life I lived before this was in no way me making the same decisions, as my parents so eloquently put it. I had never made the decision to blend a family. I didn't care about anyone but me and my kids. I had never made the decision to do things God's way, the right way. I was living a reckless life full of promiscuity. I had never made the decision to die to myself and walk a journey with another flawed human being. Before, I was selfish and controlling. But when I married Ace I was different, they just couldn't see past my past mistakes. I thought all I needed was love to make my marriage work, but it was deeper than that. Respect, peace, loyalty, and commitment is what I needed.

Most of the pressure I put on my father about certain things needed to be shared with my mothers as well. That's a tough thing for me to say, but it is genuinely how I feel. What would've been nice is for my mothers to introduce me to the woman in Proverbs 31. I knew I needed to be able to cook, clean, give my husband sex, and pick my battles, but what I really needed to learn was deeper than that.

I thought I was ready to be someone's wife and I still had so much to learn. I didn't need to be protected, I needed to be properly educated.

Knowing that I wholeheartedly gave marriage a try is enough for me to walk away feeling like I did the best with what I had at the moment.

The gems I picked up along the short journey will carry me further this time. That isn't to say I won't screw up somewhere down the road, but my decision making will happen from a healed place. Things I was attracted to before don't excite me anymore. I deserve a healthy Godly love and that's the only thing I am willing to accept moving forward.

CHARM IS DECEITFUL, AND BEAUTY
IS VAIN, BUT A WOMAN WHO FEARS
THE LORD IS TO BE PRAISED.

PROVERBS 31:30

Chapter 10

SUNSHINE, RAIN, AND TEARS

I CAN'T talk about the sunny days and not mention the cloudy days. After dealing with infidelity, lack of trust, and misunderstandings, Ace and I decided to call it quits. The process wasn't a messy one, because we both understood what needed to take place. We gave up on the marriage, but he's always had my back. He's that kind of man.

The day Ace moved out of the house was really hard on me emotionally. We were already talking about him moving out, but no real plans were being made. We were becoming toxic for one another and we knew something had to change immediately. I'm glad he had the strength to make that move because I didn't have it at the time. It was the weekend of my birthday when he told me he picked up shifts to work all weekend and he wouldn't be celebrating with me. This was the time that he also let me know he had found an apartment and that he would start moving that same weekend. There was a sadness that came over me that I cannot explain, but I kept it to myself. I knew he was off work in the upcoming days so I waited. Waited for nothing.

He hadn't packed a single box here at the house, so when his next off days came I was hoping for time with him. I asked him if he was coming to the house or going to his apartment and his exact words were, "There's really no real reason for me to come back there tonight." I lost it. All I could hear was he didn't want to be around me. He wasn't being mean, there was just no real reason for him to drive 45 minutes back over here that night. I had been begging for quality time when I should've been preparing myself for the things that were about to take place. My soul was starving for affection and attention and either he didn't feel it or he just simply didn't care.

I cried myself to sleep every night for a couple of weeks. I couldn't sit at my desk at work without crying. How could this be happening to me? My faith was depleted for a while. I had reached my breaking point and I let all of my raw emotions spill out in an unhealthy way. He had stopped taking my calls and wouldn't respond to any of my text messages. I made sure to let him know that he was a horrible person for leaving us. Why would you awaken this thing and walk away from it without any real resolve? We had never been to marriage counseling, there was no real conversation about what was expected when he moved away, and the fact that we had not exhausted every option bothered me. We had only been married for three years and we were already giving up. Because all of my emotions were so raw I couldn't even see the beauty in hitting the reset button. I had expectations and this was not the way I saw things going. Every time I would get Ace on the phone I was angry. My controlling nature needed answers immediately. Was there someone else? Why don't you love me anymore? I neglected the fact that I knew it takes him time to process things and information overload made him shut down. Raw emotions have no place in these situations. They will have you searching for things you already have the answers to. I knew in my heart that our marriage had reached a brick wall. I knew he was unhappy because I was unhappy. We stopped going on dates, the sex was totally gone, the trust was shattered, but here I was hoping for reconciliation. Was this unconditional love? It took a lot of tears and reflecting to be at peace with what my marriage would become. My thoughts had begun to shift from emotional to realistic and logical.

What happens if I never get the closure I need from Ace? I've asked Ace what his plans are. Are we separating to divorce or to eventually continue what we started? Some days he would give me a straight answer or no answer at all. During this time he was still supporting us financially. He dropped tons of groceries and necessities off when we needed it. If I needed anything he provided it without question. It was clear that he loved me and had my back. I'll never take that away from him. He was just emotionally unavailable and it was killing me.

It's extremely hard to grieve when you have no clue what to grieve about and being in the dark is very uncomfortable. Your mind will start to play tricks on you. In the exact moment you find yourself in the dark, thank God from the depths of your soul. I was in a full meltdown and thanking God for working it out at the same time. The emotions were still there. Sadness started to become a very familiar one, but I fought hard to ward off doubt. I was waiting around to hear from Ace's mouth what his actions already said loud and clear. I think I was prepared for either option, but I felt stupid for waiting around for an answer. The answer was always there, I just didn't like it. I genuinely believe Ace loved me and he thought he could do life with me, but people are allowed to change their minds along their journey. As much as it hurt, I had to respect it.

The pain became too much to bear and I began to feel numb. There was no way it would work out now. My Family structure was too flawed in itself to take the weight of my burdens. Everybody was so disconnected that we forgot to simply be there for each other's darkest moments without judgement or ego. We had begun to tolerate one another. I began to neglect my health, my family, and my relationship all for the sake of the business. Yes, we had to work and families had to eat, but there has to be a family in the first place. So to add to my issues at home, work and family became another heavy weight.

The vibe at the office was off and it felt uncomfortable. I was dealing with a lot and because the family dynamic was off my parents and I started to clash. We had our own personal family issues to deal with so there was no room for my marital issues. There was no way to separate work from personal life in our situation and eventually I was fired by my dad. Initially I was angry because how could he do this knowing my situation was already heavy? I no longer trusted anyone. Although my heart was broken, I understand that situations that arise in my life are always deeper than what's on the surface. It took me until well after I had children to realize that. I feel like I was blessed with daughters for a reason. God gave me these beautiful souls to nurture. I was given the task to nurture the soul of a girl who would one day become a woman. To me, this is an assignment that I simply cannot fumble. I was placed in my family for a reason and if this uncomfortable move is what needs to be done to solidify that core family structure I was prepared.

I felt a sense of relief once I was let go from the family business. I felt at peace and I was able to think and properly heal my heart and soul. The voices of people were turned down and God's voice was amplified. Detaching yourself from others to find yourself will feel like betrayal, but if it is indeed a necessary step in your process then you have to take it. The tears I shed were necessary. I no longer want my tears to be associated with pain. They helped cleanse me. Healing was necessary for the next season of my life.

JOURNAL ENTRY: AUGUST 29TH, 2021

Morning time for me used to be rough, but now my mornings have become my sacred space. I cry here, write in my journal, I spend time with God, my spirit is just calm. It's in those moments that I am assured that I will be ok. I literally had to stop worrying about tomorrow. The minute I stopped worrying and started being diligent in my work and left the rest up to Him, everything started to work out. I mean everything. I stopped worrying so He made my worries less.

Today I was fired from my job of almost 8 years. I don't understand why my dad has to be in control of everything. It's so unfair because I did everything the way he wanted me to with this job. Even if I didn't agree with something I gave him my opinion but the job was always done his way. It's his company so I don't have a choice, but my personal life is something he will never have control of. It doesn't matter how he dresses it up, it's a form of control. I know it so well because I am him. To hear my dad say we can't have a personal relationship and do business together is hurtful. We can, it just requires him to mentally transition into the fact that his daughter is a full-grown adult and her personal life is hers.

I'm 35 and I just realized that my daddy issues go deeper than I thought. His need to "protect" me slowly evolved into a form of control and it hurts to even say that. New marital issues for me were his cue to imply that I was going down the same path and making the same choices in men. But going down the same road would be running back to the streets. Instead I'm running towards my purpose and I'm passionate about it. If my marriage doesn't last, it ain't the end of the world. What should be more important is the lessons I learned along the way. I'm not scorned, I'm confused. The gift God has given me ain't for my dad or anyone else to understand. I am not making the same choices I made in my early 20s. My evolution as a woman and a mother in itself is enough. I take care of my children, I found someone who I thought I wanted to spend the rest of my life with and we got married. So what if we started having problems? I will never apologize to anyone for falling in love and getting married. I have experienced love in its purest form and I know what I deserve. I have been in some bad situations and when I made the decision to change that and do life with someone wholeheartedly, it still wasn't good enough for him. I am evolving as a woman and all he can see is the past mistakes. The trials won't stop and neither will the mistakes. I'm built for this journey. The pain I'm going through is something I don't know how to deal with, but I'm trying. I can't live my life for anyone but the creator.

Chapter 17

THE SOUL OF THE HEALER

YOUR *mind is the very center of your soul,* if you can master your thoughts and emotions you will master your soul.

I had begun to feel like a failure and I knew I had to heal myself on a deeper level. Deep healing was the only way I could step into my true identity, but the lack of discipline had me stuck. Depression had to leave and suicidal thoughts could be no more. It got so bad for me that I began to think my daughters would be better off without me. That was a very dangerous way to think. There were some areas within me that needed to be addressed. I was at war with my core and if I didn't heal it, I was bound to damage it. The heart is such a sacred place and I let too many people that were not worthy occupy that space. I allowed fear and insecurity to seep into my heart and they almost poisoned me. I was hurt, bad. The journey healing my core gave me a different level of courage. The devil had convinced me that I was a coward. I wasn't afraid to address the devil anymore. Why should i be? He's the one that's already defeated.

I'm learning to let go of the things I can't control, God will always be there and the encounters I have had with Him have been life changing.

The pain that I've experienced was always going to birth my purpose. At the beginning of my journey I vowed to always do things my way and I have done just that. My father and I reached an odd phase in our father daughter relationship. During a very heated discussion he made a statement, "I don't know what our relationship will be."

"We will just have to do the work," I said to him. "I think the one thing you have to know is that I am going to walk my own path and do life my way. I value some parts of your wisdom, and those things I apply to my life. If I don't agree with it I just leave it." He responded, "Can we agree that your path hasn't always been the right one?" I paused for a moment. "The journey hasn't always looked 'right,' but it's mine." I have stood ten toes down against my demons with God leading me and I have embraced the ugly parts of the journey. The journey looks wrong, but as I continue to grow, my mentality evolves. I've extracted the lessons and I am stepping into the place God wants me to be. I understand my father's position, but God's voice just became louder than his. God had to get me by myself so that I could hear only His voice. Every relationship takes time and work and my father will always be worth it.

The questions that burned deep on the inside of me were not connected to any title or achievement. My identity wasn't connected to things, It was truly a, "Who are you?" type of thing. Wondering what I am here for woke me up plenty of nights. Who was I?

The day I filed for divorce crushed me. My faith in love was restored months before I filed, but to complete such an official task set me back emotionally. It was the ending of a beautiful union and the beginning of my soul work. I was intentional about the work I would do on myself. I made it my mission to fall deeply in love with myself, but most importantly, to heal.

Separation from Ace and isolation from my family revealed things to me. It forced me to forgive and love unconditionally. It taught me to lean on God and find solace in His presence only. If it disturbed my peace I had to let it go. I pleaded with God to examine every part of my heart that was rotten so that I could properly heal. The soul of a healing vessel is a sacred place. My soul has been resilient in the face of adversities. It has gone through large amounts of trauma, both self-inflicted and directly inflicted by other people. But just as the soul takes care of me I must nurture it. That means I have to be gentle with myself when I mess up. If I make a bad decision I don't let it consume me. It doesn't define me. I am still worthy after the mistakes, no matter how many they are. Mistakes along your journey don't make you incapable of being the leader of your path. Those life experiences can be turned into some of the greatest lessons. There are certain lessons that only God can teach you.

The amazing thing about my walk with God is that I'm allowed to be vulnerable with Him. Even after I've cried my eyes out to Him, full of shame, He still sees the greatness in me. He's proven to me that He trusts me on so many levels. He isn't afraid to get in the dirt with me. After years of getting it wrong but finding myself along the way, He still trusts me with my journey. That in itself is enough for me to unapologetically walk with my head held high.

The moment I fully surrendered myself over to God my purpose became so clear. The tests won't stop. I just get through them a little easier being able to hear God's voice for myself. Trials look different for everyone so I can't give you a play by play of what yours will look like. In my case it required isolation and separation. The best thing I could've done for myself is embrace the good, the bad, and the ugly. Own it. By all means learn and grow, but own it. Celebrate the wins and stop to smell the roses every now and then. Those are the moments when you plant your feet in what your foundation should be. I have had two families for my whole life. I've lived in both homes, experienced all of my parents' journeys with them, but I've always known I would do things my own way. Good or bad, the decision would be mine. As I have gotten older those decisions are rooted in different things. Behaviors that I had in my early 20s can't come with me in this next chapter of my life. The desires I had then I don't have now. I am finally finding myself and although it feels lonely at times, it is beautiful.

Sarah Jakes Roberst said it best, "I am starting over, but I'm not starting from scratch." I have more tools now. My outlook on life is different. I'm still going to make mistakes but I'm older and wiser. I appreciate your wisdom, dad, but I have some of my own now. I want my parents to understand that the foundation they have set for me is unmatched. Although my journey doesn't look pretty and I didn't always get it right, it was my journey. I stayed true to myself, and the main thing is that I am not the person I used to be. I have begun to reflect on how important family is. I went a little deeper and discovered that healthy family relationships are what has to take place for my peace. I have to protect the peace at all costs.

When Ace moved out I experienced a range of raw emotions. I had been through some pretty traumatic experiences with men in my life, but this was my first time with my husband. There is no rule book that comes with marriage, so we must know that there isn't one that comes with separation and divorce. When you work with family it is extremely difficult to separate the business from personal. The luxury I thought I had was the fact that I worked with my family, so on the days I wasn't my best self the space was still safe. My energy was off and it was visible. One day I was angry. The next day I was hurt. I had been hit before, but these blows felt different. Not only was the space unsafe for my vulnerability, it was also already saturated with so many of our own personal issues and there was no room for my personal trauma.

The changes that were taking place in my life were taking control of me. I didn't like who I was becoming so I went to find a therapist. It hit me all at once and I soon realized that my healing is my responsibility. I wanted to break cycles and do things my way so I had to take control of my own stuff. The next part of my journey requires a healed soul. I started to do the work.

My life was taking a shift and in order to keep moving forward I had to feel every single emotion. I needed to feel it, identify what it was, spend time figuring out why it was a trigger for me, then move on and tackle the next thing. I could not fumble this opportunity to see myself because with self-reflection comes growth and new-ness. My soul needed to feel that. The emotions I experienced when my husband moved out were not always pleasant. The night time was the worst time for me, I spent hours balled up under my covers soaking my pillows with tears. After a full night of that I had to pull it together for the kids the following morning. Like clockwork I cried. I felt a range of things, but most importantly I felt misunderstood. I felt myself snapping at work and I just started to feel heavy. My personal issues were always at the forefront, but add family issues on top and the load is almost unbearable. To take it a step further your work is your family and now the weight becomes too much to handle.

Now that I am a mother I understand the weight that a parent feels when trying to guide and protect their child. I am barely stepping into the teen phase with daughters, but what I can't subscribe to is this notion that I have the blueprint for their life. The plan I have set for my motherhood journey is to guide and nurture my daughters, but to keep in mind that at some point the individual in them will flourish. One day they will have gained their own wisdom through life experiences and I won't need to say as much. I may not always agree with certain parts of their journeys, but it will be their own. All of their life lessons may not come from me and that is ok. One day they will hear God's voice for themselves and He is the ultimate leader. They will discover new things and new ways that work for them. When they reach my age I may not need to be what I was for them when they were 14, 21, 25. I will need new tools to parent young adults transitioning into adults. The decision to heal myself is at the top of my biggest accomplishments list.

While you are breaking generational curses you will be met with much resistance, but stay the course. There will be times when you feel like you're on an island all by yourself. Try not to get discouraged when you feel like you've taken steps back during the process.

Our souls carry the weight of an entire generation looking to us to bring restoration to families and relationships. The generations before us laid the foundation, but it is up to us to continue the healing work and add to it. The only way you can properly add to it is to heal the deepest wounds. We leave the deepest wounds untreated and they infect us so badly.

My life changed when I learned that our opportunities don't come from people. We get let down by humans because we link up with people with opportunity in mind. There isn't one person walking this earth that can supply you with more than God can.

Try not to let the stressors of life dictate the way you feel about yourself. Sometimes the kitchen goes messy, sometimes the laundry piles up. The girls don't complete their chores every day. Normally I would fuss about it and go into these ego driven rants, but at what cost? The last thing I wanted to do was sacrifice our relationship. I make a daily effort to cultivate their hearts, their minds, and their souls. If 100% of my focus was on the girls' appearance, making sure everything was prim and proper at all times, I wouldn't have time to connect with them. I care more about how they treat themselves first and the type of human beings they become. I allow them space to vent, I allow them space to breathe, but most importantly, I'm gentle and patient with myself. Mothers are much more than house keepers. We are soul keepers and it is such a beautiful feeling to value souls more than things. On the days I don't cook I don't beat myself up. We ate takeout but the conversation I had with my daughters felt liberating. I got a few steps closer to learning their love language.

I am slowly starting to reach for the things that I want. I used to be so lonely and I would long for that affection that I once felt with each of my kids' fathers before the betrayal. I prayed many nights for God to take those things away from me. Not necessarily the sex, but just the desire to want someone because that is what caused me so many heartaches in the past. I just wanted the loneliness to go away. I won't say I have accepted the fact that I am alone right now, but I will say that I work hard daily for my healing.

Happiness comes from within, but we slip up sometimes. We get comfortable in the marriage, comfortable in the way the family dynamic has been, and we lose ourselves. I got too comfortable letting another flawed human be solely responsible for my happiness. I have been in numerous relationships in my life, and I blamed each one of them for making me unhappy. Going through a breakup in my early 20s is much different than being 35 and going through a divorce. Today I feel good, but tomorrow I may feel like my world is crashing. There are days when the pressure is heavy on me and I almost fold. I'm not kind to myself. I have to be honest about it because it's that real.

Your mind is the center of your soul. Your soul is and will forever be the most important part of your existence. That's why It's dangerous to let your thoughts run wild for too long while you are in the midst of a storm. There are days when I have to stand in the mirror and give myself pep talks, because I am certainly my biggest critic. Depression and anxiety are rooted in lies and if you allow them to, they will poison your mind. Life had to happen to me, otherwise I would be out here doing the same things I was doing ten years ago.

Healing is a process that is seemingly never ending. Be prepared to put the work in every single day. Be still. Spend time in God's presence and He will show you how to navigate through the journey.

JOURNAL ENTRY
1-3-2022

Today I met the person I will spend the rest of my life with.

Although the journey to find you left me feeling abandoned, I knew I had to keep searching.

I was so hype and wanted to tell someone, but this is the kind of love you hide. I've worked too hard to let just anybody have access to it. This one I'll keep to myself.

This love ain't a secret, it's just too sacred...

EPILOGUE

"DO NOT LOSE SIGHT OF YOUR EXISTENCE
BECAUSE YOU HAVE HAD A FEW SEASONS
OF BARENESS. LIFT YOUR HEAD, LOOK AHEAD,
YOU HAVE SO MUCH MORE TO GIVE."

KIRDES SIRRAH

ACKNOWLEDGEMENTS

To my heavenly father: Writing this book forced me to strengthen the most important relationship in my life and I'm grateful for it. God, I know you are the giver of every gift I possess and I aim to make you proud. Everything I do will always be for your glory. You know the depths of me and you still see me as valuable.

Ace:
What we shared was beautiful. Your heart is pure gold and I will always thank God for our union because it taught me a lot about live, love and myself. You're a real one and there will never be another Ace. (smooth as Tennessee whisky) I will ALWAYS love you.

To my children:
You guys are my biggest blessing and my greatest accomplishment. I truly believe God gave me you to expose me to patience, love, and forgiveness. I am forever indebted to you and my love for you will always be unconditional.

Maddison:
Thank you for introducing me to motherhood. When you came into this world I had no clue who I was as a woman let alone a mother.

Your quiet spirit won't always be understood, but it doesn't need to be because that's what makes you special. I love your creative mind, you really are a cool kid. I can't wait to have your art hanging in the house and brag to everybody about my baby, the artist!!! You are most certainly my spirit twin and the older you get the more things I learn from you. You've taught me how to love and forgive on a deeper level and for that I am grateful. I enjoy the nights we sit in my room laughing about crazy stuff. My first baby forever. Purrrr

Kennedy:

Big Ken, not the little one!!Lol

Being a leader won't always come easy. (Bossy self. Lol) You will face problems at every corner. Face them head on and don't let it break you. I really laugh when I watch how motherly you are to me and your sisters. That's the leader in you. I pray that I'm on this earth long enough to see you become whoever God wants you to be. I pray that he helps you see your purpose early in life. Keep your kind spirit, but still check em if they test you!

Rhileey:

Poooooooooo!!!!! Where do I start? You're really the inspiration behind this book… What I love most about you is your uniqueness, your strong will and your jokes. You're definitely the funniest girl I know…I want you to know that everybody won't understand you, but that is not your problem, it's theirs. God will place the right people in your life and you will know who they are. Always be kind and respectful while staying true to yourself.

Ashton:

I believe God placed you in my life for a reason. I haven't watched you grow from birth, but I am blessed to be able to watch you grow into womanhood. That HBCU is lucky to have you out there. Live life your way, baby. The goals you want to attain in life are reachable. You may suffer a bit, just make sure that suffering is connected to your purpose. Be persistent and consistent and always seek God's face. You'll never be alone. It ain't on you, IT'S IN YOU!

Mesiah:
Son, You are in high school now and I cannot wrap my mind around it. Watching you transition from a boy to a teen has been amazing. You've done so gracefully (I'm sure there are things we don't know about. Lol) I'm grateful that you were placed into our lives. The girls really consider you a brother and you will always be a son to me! Mrs. Porcia loves you forever.

To my nieces and nephews:
I haven't been the best auntie lately, but the love I have for you runs deep. Aunt Porcia will always be a safe space. ―

Daddy, you are my first love and your wisdom has set the foundation for who I am. Not only have you taught me to be a fearless business woman, but you made sure to teach me to be a woman of integrity and to always make sure my heart is in the right place. I know it might be a little difficult to see me walk this journey, but I want you to know I'm built for it. You built me for it. God will take care of me like He always has. Love you deep…

Mama Deshon, thank you for your endless prayers and encouraging words.
You made sure me and Nerra were rooted in the word and it was the best thing you could have done for us. Because of your teachings I am confident. I am able to pass that on to my daughters and they are falling right in line. We are daughters of the Most High. I love you.

Mama Tam, I've seen you go through some pretty rough battles and your strength is so admirable. You are truly an angel on earth…You are the reason I'm strong. Blending families ain't for the weak, but you've done it with so much grace and class. You are the backbone to this whole thing! I love you forever and always.

Aunt Princess, where do I start?? Lol. You are the funniest woman I know! Thank you for comforting me in some of my lowest moments. You have been there to wipe tears and you have made this process easier. Your presence and wisdom mean more to me than anything anyone could ever physically give me. There were times when I could only pay you with food stamps and a child support card and you still showed up to help with my babies. Thank you for walking this motherhood journey with me every step of the way. I owe you so much. It's happening, auntie…

Ms J: I am so grateful for you. Not only was I blessed with the most understanding nanny for my Rhileey poo, I gained a mother in you as well. Thank you for always loving me with a Godly love. We bout to be eating Cheerios and almonds in a mansion soon. LOL… Love you for life…

Uncle Joe, thank you for being the best uncle to all of us and thanks for sharing Aunt P with me!

To my grandmothers:
Sandra and Cornelia, both of you set the foundation and I would not be who I am if it weren't for your unconditional love and prayers. Yall are the reason I exist. I owe y'all SO MUCH!! Just hold on.

To my sisters:
Sonya, our love runs deep. Our babies will grow up with a special kind of love because of our bond. It ain't always been pretty, but you my dawg for life. (Love you, Agent Hurd)

Tiffany, them soul cleansing conversations helped me stay sane. Late night tears and early morning laughs are something I hope we can do forever. (It was an honor to have your child. LOL) Your decision to heal yourself inspired me to do the same. Love you.

Nerra, you were my first best friend. You have the greatest success story of all time. You raised a Black man and you did it gracefully.

Tia, you show up every single time and you do it with no hesitation. You're a rare breed baby girl and I can't wait to ball with you. You understand the ratchet part of me the most. Thank you for being you and allowing me to be myself. (Now leave that side door open...you know the rest.) Lol

Chantal, you are the epitome of a virtuous woman. Love you.

To my only brother, David, you my baby too. I love you with every ounce of my being. Keep shining, king.

To My sister cousins:
Latonya, Raeana, and Leo.

I am so grateful for this beautiful thing called sisterhood. There is truly no group like the 5 of us. We're built different. Who I am is because of yall.

Denekia, you and your journey inspire me in so many ways. Life gets in the way, but we are locked in for life.

To my friends, Chris and Fiona Parker, and Brandon Wheeler and Meka Wright. Yall are some rare finds and what a lucky person I am to have yall in my life!! Y'all get me. I love yall so much.

Uncle Theland and Auntie B: I'm truly inspired and I love the way y'all love each other. Going through a separation wasn't easy and yall always met me with such kind words, but most importantly, yall lead by example. (Unc, working out is NOT a piece of cake. Lol)

To my woes: Jaz, Sam, Ebs, Sarah, and Stace, I absolutely thank God for putting you ladies in my life. We all have our own lives so we can't connect as often, but when we do, the love and laughter we share always puts me back in a good space. Almost 20 years of friendship down and forever to go...

PORCIA MANN

To be completely healed is a beautiful goal, but it can oftentimes feel impossible to attain. It's a goal we all work daily to accomplish and Porcia is no exception. Intentional healing is talked about throughout her new book "A Healer's Journey to Healin", a memoir that takes the reader on the journey Porcia has traveled for the last 35 years.

In "A Healer's Journey to Healing", Porcia bares her soul to readers with the hopes of influencing a generation to heal. During the past couple of years she has endured indescribable heart ache, while dealing with the stresses of the pandemic and the unfair treatment of people of color. Porcia has anchored herself in God's word and pours her experiences into her writing.

"Writing has always been therapy for me. It's my way to do a brain dump. This is a gift that I am thankful for. I started out writing poetry when I was 13 years old. I would rather be judged a thousand times on a book than for someone to pick apart my poetry. That's a sacred space for me. What I am doing with this book is for the masses."

Chapters like "Industry baby" give the readers insight on what Porcia's life was like growing up in the entertainment industry with celebrity parents then turning around and working in the same industry. The book ends with "The Healer's Soul", a chapter that takes the reader on Porcia's journey through divorce and divine healing.

She prides herself on being an intentional mother. "My children are my motivation, and I work hard daily to make them proud. Honestly, I am the student and they are the most patient teachers."

After a few years of pain, Porcia has emerged as a triumphant and wiser woman who has discovered her true purpose in life. That is to talk about God's grace and mercies through her life experiences.

"Your purpose is already inside of you, you just have to get connected to the creator and find out what it is you're supposed to be doing on this earth. That is my goal with this book. First, to let the world know that God's love is real, and lastly to let people know that there is greatness in you. Unlock it and go be great."